A Library of American Puritan Writings
THE SEVENTEENTH CENTURY

•

Series editor: Sacvan Bercovitch

VOLUME 16

The Soules Humiliation

By Thomas Hooker

AMS PRESS
NEW YORK

THE
SOVLES
HVMILIATION.

Iob 22. Verſe 29.
And He ſhall ſave the humble Perſon.

The third Edition.

LONDON,
Printed by *T. Cotes* for *Andrew Crooke,* and
Philip Nevill. 1640.

Library of Congress Cataloging in Publication Data

Hooker, Thomas, 1586–1647.
  The soules humiliation.

  (A Library of American Puritan writings; v. 16)
  Photoreprint of the 3d ed., 1640, published by
A. Crooke, and P. Nevill, London.
  1. Conversion–Early works to 1800. I. Title. II.
Series: Library of American Puritan Writings; v. 16.
BT780.H66   1981   248.2'4   78-293
ISBN 0-404-60816-7

Reprinted from the edition of 1640, London.

MANUFACTURED IN THE UNITED STATES
OF AMERICA

THE
SOVLES HVMILIATION.

Luke 15. Verſ. 14,15,16,17,18,&c.

14. *And when he had ſpent all, there aroſe a mightie Famine in that land, and he began to be in want,*

15. *And he went and joyned himſelfe to a citizen of that country, and he ſent him into his fields to feed Swine.*

16. *And he would faine have filled his belly with the huskes that the ſwine did eate: and no man gave them unto him.*

17. *And when he came to himſelfe, he ſaid, How many hired ſervants in my Fathers houſe have bread enough, and to ſpare, and I periſh with hunger.*

18. *I will ariſe, and goe to my Father, and will ſay unto him, Father, I have ſinned, &c.*

THat a poore ſinner might come. and be partaker of the precious merits and death of our Saviour and receive comfort thereby ; There are two things conſiderable. Firſt, a fitting & enabling of the ſoule for Chriſt. Secondly, an implantation of the Soule into Chriſt. For

how-

howsoever it is true there is abundance of mercy,
and infinite merit in Christ : yet unlesse the Soule
be fitted and enabled by the hand of faith, to lay
hold upon Christ; hee shall never receive comfort
from him, be his necessities never so many, and his
misery never so grievous. Therefore *Iohn Baptist* was
sent to prepare the way, that all those mountaines
of pride might be laid low, and all the ditches filled
up, and all the crooked things might be made
straight, and all rough things might be made
smooth, that there may be a way for Christ. The
meaning is this : The heart of a man is the high-
way wherein Christ comes. Now there are mountaines of pride and untoward stoutnesse of heart,
and many windings and turnings, and devices which
the heart hath, by reason of many lusts that are in it.
This fitting and preparing, is nothing else but the
taking away of that knottie knarlinesse of the heart,
and that pride, and all such cursed corruptions, that
the doore may be set open, and the heart made ready that the King of glory may come in.

The heart being thus fitted and enabled, then followes humiliation : for the breaking of the heart is
not all that God hath to doe with a poore sinner,
though the Lord wound the heart of a sinner, and
run him through, yet the heart will be starting aside,
and will not goe out to Christ. Therefore I shall
now speake of humiliation of the spirit, yet before
I come to it, give mee leave to lay open two passages.

   1. The necessitie of this worke, it must needs be.
   2. The nature of this worke.

First, it is necessary that the soule should be thus
humbled

humbled ; for humiliation pares away all felfe-fuf-
ficiencie from the foule by compunction : the Lord
breakes the heart, and wearies it with finne, and then
the foule will be no more drunke, nor loofe, nor vaine,
no more foolifh, nor diffembling, nor hating of
Gods fervants, nor ufe no more falfe weights : by humiliation the Lord plucks away the confidence in a
mans priviledges, and all his good performances, and
all his duties, by which he is ready to fhelter himfelfe, and by which hee thinkes to get fome fuccour
and comfort to his own foule. Now as fin fhall not
rule in the heart, fo the Lord will make the finner fee,
that whatfoever hee hath and doth, can never helpe
him, except the Lord Iefus come downe from heaven by his mighty power. For the further opening of
thefe, you muft know that there are thefe two maine
lets, which hinder the comming of faith into the
foule, and which keepe a man from beleeving in
Chrift, that Chrift may have poffeffion of him.

First, when the foule is taken up with a fecure _{I.}
course, and refts it felfe well apaid in his owne pra- Let of Faith.
ctifes, & therfore it never feeth any need of a change,
nor never goes out for a change : now while he lives
thus, and bleffeth himfelfe in his finne, it is impoffible that ever the Soule fhould receive faith, or ever
by the power of faith repaire to Chrift upon thefe
termes : for ever where faith comes, it works a change,
all the old things are done away, and become new,
he is new in heart and life ; now the fecure finner
that feeth no need of a change, will never fee need of
faith, nor labour for it ; and if the Minifters of God
bid fuch a man to leave his finne, and to pray in his

family,

family,and forlake his finfull practiles,and to fanctifie the Lords day, and take up new courfes, he thinks
they bid him to his loffe:now by that time the Lord
hath taken away this let, and burthened the Soule
marvellous extreamely, and faith, is it well that you
live in drunkenneffe,and in covetoufneffe,in cheating
in lying,and the like,then take your fins and get you
downe to hell with them; thus the Lord is forced to
breake the heart : then a poore finner begins to fee
where now he is, and now he faith, and is this true,
then I am the moft miferable creature under heaven,
and except I be otherwife, it had beene good for me
if I had never been borne,by this time the foule fees
neede of a change : therefore, as they faid. *Men and*
brethren what ſhall wee doe,we have been thus and thus,
but if we reft here it will be our ruine for ever, oh,
what fhall we doe. Thus the foule comes to a reft-
leffe diflike of it felfe, and faith,I muft either be o-
therwife, or elfe I am but a damned man for ever.

  When the foule is thus refolved that it muft of neceffitie change, & there is no dallying with the Lord
nor with himfelfe, and this heart muft be altered,and
this courfe muft be amended. When it fees that it
muft change, it begins to improve all meanes to fee
if he can poffibly doe it by his owne ftrength,and by
his meanes ufing, as if the foule did fay, good Lord
cannot my wit compaffe it, and cannot my prayers
worke it,and though I am a finfull wretched man,yet
I will be no more drunke, nor uncleane, nor the like :
but by prayer, and hearing, and fafting, I will labour
to mend all in this kinde; will not thefe duties doe
the deed?this very refting in a mans felfe-fufficiency
           doth

Acts 2.37.

doth marvelloufly croffe and hinder the worke of Faith, for this is the nature of Faith; It goes out of it felfe, and fetcheth a principall of life, grace, and power from another. The Soule apprehends it felfe miferable, and it falls upon the arme of Gods mercy, and meerly goes out to God for fuccour. Now for a man to fetch all from without, and it to feeke for fufficiencie from himfelfe, thefe two cannot ftand together they are profeffely croffe one to another; and therefore after the Lord hath made the Soule fee an abfolute neceffitie of a change, and now the Soule feeth an utter impoffibilitie in himfelfe, to change or alter himfelfe, then he is content to go to Chrift for grace and power. Thus Humiliation pares away all a mans priviledges, and all his hearing, and praying, &c. not, that a man muft ufe thefe no more, but hee muft not reft upon them for ftrength to help and fuccour himfelfe withall. As it is with the graft; Firft, it muft be cut off from the old ftocke. 2. It muft be pared and made fit for the implantation into another. So the Soule being cut off from fin, then Humiliation pares it, and makes it fit for the ingrafting into Chrift. Thus you fee this worke is abfolutely neceffary.

But what is this Humiliation of heart ? It is thus much. When the Soule upon fearch made, defpaires of all helpe from it felfe : hee doth not defpaire of Gods mercy, but of all help from himfelfe and fubmits himfelfe wholy to God, the foule ftrikes fale and falls under the power of Iefus Chrift, and is content to be at his difpofing.

In this defcription let me difcover thefe three particular paffages.

First,

What Humiliation is.

First, the sinner that is now wounded and apprehensive of his own misery, makes out for some succor and remedy else-where, but he doth not go to Christ.

2. Secondly, when he useth all meanes that he can, he seeth no helpe at all, nay, he utterly despaires of finding any succour from himselfe or from the creature.

3. Then the soule despairing of all succour in himselfe it fals downe at the Throne of Grace, and saith, if the Lord will! damne him he may, and if he will save him he may, which as yet he cannot see, but he resolves to waite upon God for mercy; hee submits himselfe to the Lord, and is content to be at his disposing.

For the first part of the Discription that the Soule seeketh for remedy else-where, and not from Christ. This is expreft here in the 15.verse of this Chapter. The Prodigall would needs have his Portion, and he would not ever be a slave in his fathers family : well he hath it, and gone he is, and he hath spent all, and when all was gone there fell a great famine in the Land; and what did he then? He would not now ryot any more as he had done, because Povertie pinched him in this kinde, but he turnes good husband, and is content to use any meanes for his maintenance, and he would make hard shift before he would go home to his Father, and therefore he joynes himselfe to a Citizen of the Countrey, &c.

This Prodigall is a true picture of every poore distressed sinner that hath ryoted away his Time, yet at laft when the venome of sinne begins to scorch and pierce his soule, and he is famished for want of Gods favour, and the wrath of God pursues him, and a desperate sorrow seaseth upon his heart, and he is wearied and burthened and tried with his sinne, and sees that he hath no helpe, he sets all his wits to worke to see if he can tell which way to succour himselfe in these his grievances, and though he will not take up any base courses as he had done, but proves a good husband and useth all meanes to succour himselfe: so the Doctrine from hence is this.

A sinner naturally in his trouble and distresse seeks *Doctrine.* for succor (not from God nor from Christ) but from himselfe and from his owne abilities.

So that the soule being in this great extremitie of heart by reason of his sinne, he dares not, nay he will not meddle with sinne any more but it betakes it selfe to hearing and praying, and to other duties ordinarie and extraordinary, and by these it thinkes to be absolutely succoured. I confesse the best of Gods Saints must use these meanes, they must heare and pray, and fast, but they must not rest upon these ; it was very fit that the Prodigall should labour for his living, but not that he should not withall seeke home to his father for reliefe. So it is requisite that we should heare and pray and fast, but these should not keepe us from a father. It is the nature of man naturally to make of meanes a Saviour to himselfe : he scraps for some succour and rests upon some rotten indeavours, and because he can heare and pray and fast, he thinkes this is enough to save him, he uses not these to bring him to Christ but rests on them.

It is a naturall thing ingrafted into all man-kinde since the fall of *Adam*: as you may see by the Apostle because the Iewes were scrambling for life and happinesse from the works of the Law, therfore they could

not

not attaine it, but the Gentiles which did not seeke it from the workes of the Law, they got it : as if he had said, when they saw their anguish and trouble then they fell upon these duties of hearing and praying and fasting, and they thought that was enough in conscience, and here they tooke up their stand, this is to cleave to a man of the Countrey. And the same Apostle saith, they being ignorant of the Righteousnesse of God, sought to establish themselves in their owne Righteousnesse, &c. this they would have, here they would rest, and here they would die. In common experience we may see it : take a poore sinner that hath beene soundly awakened in the sence of his own vilenesse, what is the ground of his hope ? Oh, saith he, now the World is well amended with me, and I have not been drunke so many yeares, and I have performed these and these duties, as if that would serve the turne: this is to looke for happinesse from a mans owne duties. It is with a poore sinner as it was with *Ephraim*, when *Ephraim* saw his wound and his sickenesse, then he went to *Ashur* and to King *Iaribbe*, that is to the king of Contention or advocate, but he did not heale their wound. Therefore the lamenting Church saith *Ashur*, and the King of Egypt our gods, and wee thought wee might have hired helpe from them; but now we see there is no helpe in them : as it was in that temporall distresse, so it is in this spirituall affliction of the soule. When the soule seeth his wound and his sinne before him to condemne him, and misery prepared to plague him, and he hath (as it were) a little peepe-hole into hell, the soule in this distresse sends over to prayer and hearing and holy

service.

Rom 10,3.

Hosea 5. 13.

services, and thinkes by his wits and duties, or some such like matters to succour it selfe, and it begins to say my hearing and my prayer, &c. will not these save me? Thus the soule in conclusion rests in these duties. Though these duties be all good, honourable comfortable, yet they are no gods at all able of themselves to save us, but they are the Ordinances of God that leade us to God, yet they cannot give salvation to any that rests upon them. It is the nature of a sinfull heart to make the meanes as meritorious to salvation; yet mistake me not, these duties must be had and used, but still a man must not stay here: a man will use his bucket, but he expects water from the Well: these meanes are the Buckets, but all our comfort, and all our life and grace is onely in Christ; if you say your bucket shall helpe you, you may starve for thirst if you let it not downe into the well for water: so, though you bragge of your praying, and hearing, and fasting, and of your almes, and building of hospitals and your good deeds, if none of these bring you to a Christ, you shall die for thirst, though your workes were as the workes of an Angell.

But why doth the soule seeke for succour from it selfe, and will not goe out to Christ?

The first reason is, because the sinner (being conceived not yet to be in Christ) out of the guilt of sin dares not be so proud as to thinke that he shall have any favour at Gods hands, for the sinner being now overwhelmed with the body of death and the guilt of his abominations galling of him, and being starved by reason of his sinnes, and still his sins being before his eyes, and to this day having gotten no assurance of

1. Reason

the

the pardon of them, and God being angry againſt him, his heart ſhrinkes in conſideration of the eternall wrath of the Almighty againſt him, and he ſaith, becauſe I have deſpiſed Juſtice and abuſed Mercy, how dare I appeare before Gods Juſtice ; for feare juſtice conſume me and execute vengeance upon me, and therefore the ſoule dares not yet venture to come before God: and hence it is that the ſoule ſaith, can I not take ſome courſe of my ſelfe and doe it without Chriſt ? Muſt I needes goe and heare ? Certainly the word will condemne: and muſt I needs goe and confeſſe my ſinne? What ſhall I, a Rebell goe before a Prince ? to come before him, it is the next way to be executed and have ſome plague throwne upon me. As a Maleſactor will deviſe ſome ſhift that hee may not come before the Judge ; ſo while the ſoule may have ſome ſuccour from himſelfe and the ſtaffe is in his owne hand there is ſome hope, and he would willingly doe any thing for himſelfe ; but for the ſoule to have ſalvation out of his owne reach, and to put the ſtaffe out of his owne hand, and to hang his ſalvation upon Gods good pleaſure, whoſe love and mercy (as yet) hee was never perſwaded of. Oh this is very hard, and the heart is marvellous ſhie and carefull in this, and it is with the heart in this kinde as *Rabſhecah* ſaid to the people of Iſrael ; *If you ſay to me, is not that he, whoſe Alters you have broken downe, &c.* Thus hee laboured to plucke away the hearts of this people from truſting in the Lord : The ſoule in this kinde ſometimes ſhakes and ſhrinkes in the apprehenſion of his owne vileneſſe, and ſaith as this wretch did, have you offended him ? And doe

you

you looke for any succour from him? This argument
was very peevish and keene and yet false, for they
were the Alters of Idols, but the soule saith against
it selfe and marvellous truly : when a Minister would
perswade a man to goe to Heaven for Mercy,
the soule beginnes to reason thus with it selfe
and saith, shall I repaire to God ? Oh thats my trouble, is not he that great God whose justice, and mercie, and patience I have abused ? and is not he the
great God of heaven and earth, that hath been incensed against me ? Oh, with what face can I appeare
before him, and with what heart can I looke for any
mercy from him ; I have wronged his justice, and
can his justice pardon me ? I have abused his mercy,
and can his mercie pitie me ? what, such a wretch as
I am ; If I had never enjoyed the meanes of mercy, I
might have had some plea for my selfe, but oh, I have
refused that mercy, and have trampled the blood of
Christ under my feet; and can I looke for any mercy?
no, no, I see the wrath of the Lord incensed against
me, and thats all that I looke for: the soule rather desires the mountaines to fall upon him, that hee may
never appeare before God. Nay, I have observed
this in experience. In the horrour of heart, the soule
dare scarce reade the word of God, and for feare hee
should reade his owne neck-verse, and hee dare not
pray, for feare his prayers be turned into sinne, and so
increase his judgement: thus the soule out of the guilt
of sinne dare not seeke out to the Lord, and therefore it will use any shift to helpe it selfe without going to God.

The second Reason, why the Soule dare not seeke 2. *Reason.*
out

B 3

out to Chrift for faccour, it is this, becaufe the myfte-
ries of life and falvation through Chrift are not yet
made knowne to the Soule, the Soule being yet con-
fidered, as barely broken and wearied with the burthen of finne. Let me fay as the Apoftle doth, the
new and living way in Chrift, is not yet revealed to
the foule, and it is not yet fet open before his Eyes,
though it fhall be revealed, taking it as in this precife
confideration onely prepared for Chrift. Nay, thofe
fupernaturall Truths, namely, That the foule muft
live by another mans life, and be made holy by anothers holineffe, and be fanctified by anothers fpirit,
thefe are not yet revealed; thefe doe exceede our corrupt nature. *Adam* after his fall could not have
found out this way, if the Lord had not revealed it.
Had not the Lord Iefus Chrift that came from the
bofome of his Father, made this bofome truth
knowne, wee had never beene acquainted with it;
therefore the foule cannot come to Chrift upon thefe
termes. As our Saviour faith, *No man hath afcended up
to heaven, but hee that came downe from heaven.* Now,
this poore diftreffed finner as yet guiltie of his finne,
and yet not feeing a way revealed, and not able to af-
cend into this heavenly myfterie, becaufe it feeth no
better way, it will betake it felfe to thefe duties, that
may be done by his owne ftrength without feeking
to Chrift.

2. Reafon.   Becaufe for a man to be able, and to have a power
and principle of life, to performe duties of himfelfe,
and to pleafe God of himfelfe, it was once poffible
in the time of mans innocency; *Adam* had it, and he
might have procured Gods favour, and have kept the
                                                              Law,

Law, and have beene blessed by the Law, because the Lord had given him a stocke in himselfe, and made him able to doe it of himselfe, and wee retaine thus much of *Adams* nature, wee are loath to live of another, but we would faine be as able to doe duties as *Adam* was. And it is with every naturall man as it is with *Sampson*: hee had once Sacramentall haire, and therefore when any Temptation came, he did shake himselfe, and was able to breake strong cords, and to overcome his enemies, and when his haire was gone, he went out as at other times, and thought to doe as he had done, but the Spirit of God was gone from him : So, because *Adam* had power of himselfe to yeeld exact obedience and to please God, a naturall man makes an offer of this still, and would be doing, and he goes out and shakes himselfe, and saith, cannot my wit and my prayers, and my good meanings, and my priviledges save me, and satisfie divine Justice, must the guilt of sinne still lie upon me. Thus the soule would give content to God by his owne strength, as it is with a man that hath beene a rich Chapman, and hath had a faire stocke, but is now decayed, it is hard to bring downe the pride of this mans heart, hee is loath to be a Journey-man againe, he will be trading though it is but for pinnes: So the Lord put a stocke into *Adams* hand, and he turned bankrupt ; and yet we will be trading here for a company of poore beggerly duties, dead prayers, and cold hearings, and we think this will be sufficient. This is the disposition of the soule naturally ; So, the issue of the Point is thus much ; if the soule through the guilt of sinne dare not appeare before God, and it

knowes

knowes not how to come to God, in, and through a Mediator ; and in regard of *Adams* innocency, it needed not to goe out to another, for any power and strength, hence it is that the soule wil invent any way, & take up any course rather than come to Christ, but all the former truths are true, and therefore still this turnes the heart to deale with God in this manner.

1. *Ve*   Here you see the reason, why that opinion of some men prevailes so much, and why they rest upon their owne good works, because their hearts give such entertainement to it: it is old *Adams* nature, and every man seekes it, but if ever God draw you home to the second *Adam* Christ Iesus, he will draw you from the first *Adam*. You wonder to see a company of poore wretches, build all their comfort upon what they can do, and they will patter over a few prayers, it may be in their beds too; it is easie to consider it. Nature makes a man thus give way to himselfe in it, and no wonder though his heart is prepared for this way when it comes.

An use of instruction.   But for instruction for our selves. Doth the soule seeke out every where before it come to the Lord God ? and to the Lord Iesus Christ ? and will the Lord Iesus spare, and succour a poore sinner when he comes ? then heare, and see, and admire at the goodnesse of the Lord, that ever the Lord should vouchsafe to give entertainement to a poore sinner when he hath made so many outs. If he come home never so late, the Lord receives him when he comes. Is not this mercy, that when we have been roving and ranging, heare and there, and we have coasted this way, and that way; and never thought of Christ, nor mercy, nor

nor of his blood? I fay, is not this admirable mercy,
that the Lord Chrift, fhould receive us when wee
come, yea though we come to him laft of all? Hee
may deale with us juftly, as he did with the people
in *Ieremy, Where are thy Gods (faith the Lord) that thou
haft made thee, let them arife if they can helpe thee in the* Ier. 2. 28.
*time of thy trouble, for according to the number of thy ci-
ties are thy gods, oh Iudah.* The people made Idols and
ferved them, and when the time of trouble came, and
all their gods failed them, then they came for fuccour
to the Lord, and would faine fhelter themfelves under
his wings. Nay, faith the Lord, go to your gods that
you have loved, and let them helpe you, as if he had
faid unto them, doe you come to mee in the day of
your diftreffe, have you honoured and worfhipped
your Idols, muft they have all the honour, and I have
all the burthen, get you home to your Idols, and let
them fuccour you. Oh thinke of it and wonder. So
the Lord may juftly deale with us; we that refted
here upon our good prayers, and our hearings, and
faftings, and yet when all thefe prevaile not, but the
guilt of finne remaines, and wounds the confcience
ftill, and at laft we are forced to looke up to the Lord
Iefus Chrift, and to fay, except the Lord Iefus Chrifts
bloud purge thefe filthy hearts of ours we fhall never have helpe, and good Lord be mercifull to us.
Did you reft in thefe, becaufe there was no God in
Ifrael, and no mercy in the Almightie, that you have
refted upon your priviledges? Goe then (may the
Lord fay) doe you come to me to be faved and fuccoured? goe to your meritorious workes now, let
them cheere your heart, and pardon your finnes and

C   comfort,

comfort you, for I will not succour you at all. It were juſt with the Lord to deale thus with us, becauſe we give him the leavings, and come laſt to him. But heare is the wonder of mercies, that whenſoever we come, hee caſts us not off, yet if wee would bnt come to him, and leave theſe broken reeds, he would receive us : *Yet returne to me (ſaith the Lord :)* as if the Lord had ſaid, you ſay that all that you can doe will not ſuccour you, you have plaid the adulterers with many lovers, yet at laſt come home to mee, and beleeve in me, and ſettle your hearts upon my mercy, and whatſoever your weakeneſſe and rebellions have beene, I will ſave and ſuccour you.

The ſecond uſe is for Exhortation, ſeeing it is ſo, that we are ready to ſeek for ſuccour and reliefe from our ſelves, then let this make us watchfull againſt this deceit of our hearts. Yet I doe not diſhonour theſe ordinances, but I curſe all carnall confidence in theſe. You cleave to theſe poore beggerly duties, and (alas) you will periſh for hunger: the devill knowes this full well, and therefore he will ſinke your hearts for ever. Iudas did ſo, and hell is full of hearers, and diſſemblers, and carnall wretches, that never had hearts to ſeeke unto Chriſt in theſe duties, and to ſee the value of a Saviour in them. The devill ſlides into the heart this way unſuſpected and unſeene, becauſe he comes under a colour of duties exactly performed; but now in that the devill labours to cheate us of health and ſalvation, wee ſhould be ſo much more watchfull. This is the ſtone that thouſands have ſtumbled at; yea many that have gone a great way, in the way of life and ſalvation. For howſoever, the ſoule that is

truly

truly broken cannot be satisfied without a Chrift, yet
it may be much hindered from comming to Chrift :
but thofe that are not foundly broken and wrought
upon by the work of contrition, they are dawbed up,
and come to ruine and deftruction for ever. When
the Soule lies under the hand of God, and under his
ftroke, and a man feeth his drunkenneffe, and his bafe
contempt of God, and his grace, and all his finnes are
prefented before him ? Oh, then he voweth and pro-
mifeth to take up a new courfe, and every man will
mend one, and he begins to approve himfelfe in the
reformation of the evils committed, and then hee
neede doe no more, and now the Soule faith, well
now I fee the juftice of God is provoked, and I fee
now what finne is, and what the danger of it is, I will
have no more drunkenneffe, now I will be a fober
man, and now no more fcoffing and fcorning at thofe
that goe to heare the Word ; I will attend upon the
good Word of God my felfe, and by this time hee
thinkes thus ? What can you fay againft me ? what
can I doe more ? to heaven I muft ; all this is but a
mans felfe. Its true, this is the way, and thefe are the
very meanes, but all thefe cannot procure the pardon
of one finne, if he go no further. We have many fuch
trials : I have knowne many that have done great
workes, but never had a thought of Chrift, and never
expected falvation from him, and thus they fed upon
the huskes : and then the devill faith, you pray, and
heare, and doe duties ; fo did *Iudas* and many others
that are now in hell, then the heart feeth his vileneffe,
and he is driven to a defperate defpaire, fo that no
Minifter under heaven is able to comfort him, but he

goes away with the huske of duties, but Chrift who is the fubftance of all, and the pith of a promife is forgotten, and a Chrift in hearing, and a Chrift in prayer is not regarded, and therfore he famifheth for hunger.

The ground of the fecond Point.

Now fee the fucceffe that the Prodigall found, the cafe is cleare, he found no reliefe at all. No man gave unto him: his hungry ftomacke was not refrefhed, and his wants were not relieved; fo that now the foule of the poore man finkes unrecoverably in his mifery. And that he doth thus, confider two phrafes, firft in in the 16. verfe, *no man gave unto him.* Not, that no man gave him hnskes, for he that fed the fwine might have fed himfelfe, but the meaning is, no man gave him mans meate, if hee might have had mans meate, though never fo poore and meane, he would have beene content, but no man did give him, and hence followes the phrafe in the 17. verfe. *How many hired fervants in my fathers houfe have bread enough, and I die for hunger,* It was not becaufe he had no huskes, but becaufe he had no bread, as if he had faid, perifh I fhall, I fee no fuccour; nay, I looke for none, I may fhuffle on here for a while, but if I ftay here I am a dead man. This condition of the Prodigall, difcovers the fecond paffage in the difcription of Humiliation; So the Doctrine from hence is this:

Doctrine.

The broken hearted finner finds no helpe; nay, bee hath no hope to receive any helpe from himfelfe in the matter of juftification.

You fee the ground of the Point is cleare: The Citizen relieved him not, but hee gives himfelfe as loft, and faith; I cannot helpe my felfe, and no man will fuccour me, and therefore I perifh for hunger.

This

This is the picture of a Soule that is famished for want of the sense of Gods favour, though hee use meanes; and heareth and prayeth, and fasteth; yet he finds no good, and no found comfort in all these: not that a man must not use these meanes, but he must not rest upon these: a man must not thinke that his bucket can quench his thirst; but he fetcheth water from the fountaine with it: So, these duties are as the bucket, a man may famish for all these duties, unlesse he goe to the Fountaine of Grace, and pardon, and mercy, and in the use of all these see a neede of Christ, and goe to God for a Christ by them; these meanes must be used, but these cannot be saviours of him; these meanes must be used to bring him to a Christ, yet they cannot save him without a Christ. What was spoken temporally to *Ephraim*, it is true of the Soule spiritually : When *Ephraim* saw his wound and his sicknesse, he went to *Ashur* and King *Jarib*, but they could not helpe him, nor cure his wound. It is true, this Text mainely aimes at a temporall deliverance, but this may draw us to consider the successe that a poore Soule findes in his duties, resting upon them. When a poore soule is broken in the sight of his sinne, and weary of it; he sends downe to prayer and hearing, and the like; but these cannot succour him without Christ: and therefore the Prophet *Esay* saith, *Why lay you out your money for that which is not bread, &c.* The Lord accounts the paines of his faithfull servants good labour, and would not have them lay it out for that which is not bread. All the profits that may inrich a man, and all the honours that may advance a man; nay, all the privi-

Hosea c. 13.

Esay 55. 2.

ledges

ledges that a man hath ; as Word, Sacraments, and
Ordinances ; and that a man is baptized, and hath often come to the Lords Table ; thefe come no farther
than the very bare huske; if they goe no farther, and
have not an eye to their Saviour ; thefe are no true
bread:the horror of heart cannot be quieted, nor his
finnes pardoned, barely by thefe duties doing: the
meate of the foule, is not the bare Word, nor the
bare Sacraments;but a Chrift in all thefe : this is the
prop of the Soule : all the bare duties in the world
cannot fuccour us,if we reft upon them,without juftification through Chrift.

Phil. 3. 5, 6 7. The Apoftle *Paul*, a learned Pharifee, and a man
of an unblameable life, becaufe hee was a man of a
good life, of the Tribe of *Benjamin*, and a Iew circumcifed the eighth day ; hee thought to doe great
matters, and hee thought he had done enough ; hee
counted thefe his priviledges, gaine. What, learned
Paul ? reverend *Paul*, unblameable *Paul* ; What, not
hee goe to Heaven ? hee counted thefe his greateft
gaine ;as if he would lay down enough upon the naile
to purchafe Heaven to himfelfe:but thefe were fo far
from faving him,that he found them to be loffe. Thus
you fee that a diftreffed finner finds himfelfe helpeleffe and hopeleffe,in regard of any fufficient fuccour
in himfelfe, or the cieature, if he goe no further than
the very duty.

Now the foule finds that there is no faving fuccour to be had in thefe duties barely : I fay, he comes
to fee it by thefe three meanes.

Firft, from his owne experience that forceth him
to confeffe it.

                                                        Secondly

Secondly, from the examples of others.

Thirdly, The greatnesse of the evill that lyes upon him, makes him see an utter inabilitie to receive any good from that which he doth.

First, From his owne experience. Though he thought to take up a new course, and to performe holy duties, and thought that without all question these would save him, yet he findes now that these will not doe the deed, he hath no saving good in these; and that appeares by these three particulars. First, Hee seeth that the guilt of sinne still remaines, and the Justice of God, being unsatisfied still pursues him, though he pray, and heare, and performe many duties, as the Lord told the people, when they were sharking for their owne comfort, and they thought to give God content by their new courses. Yet the Lord tels them, *Though thou wash thee with Nitre, and* Ier. 2. 22. *take thee much sope, and though thou use all meanes of reformation, yet thy sinnes are sealed up, and thy iniquitie is marked before me.* It is with a poore sinner as the *Psalmist* saith of himselfe; *Whether shall I goe from thy Spirit, or whither shall I flie from thy presence, if I ascend up into heaven thou art there, if I lie downe in hell thou art there, if I take the wings of the morning and dwell in the utmost parts of the Sea, even thither shall thy right hand leade me, &c.* So let a poore sinner goe where he will, and doe what he can, the guilt of sin will ever be with him, it will lye dowre, and rise up, and walke with him in the way. His sins remaine unpardoned, and the wrath of God is not appeased: and hence it is that all his prayers, are but as so many inditements against him, and he dare not read the Word for feare he

Psal. 139. 7. 8. 9.

he should read his owne damnation. Nay, at every Sermon that he heares, he seeth more vilenesse in himselfe, and every Sacrament that he receives, increaseth (not his comfort but) his horror, & he thinks thus with himselfe, good Lord I have taken my bane this day for I come unpreparedly, & the Lord knows what an unfaithfull, and unbeleeving heart I have.

2. Secondly, as the guilt of sinne cannot be removed by all his duties, so his conscience cannot be quieted by all that he doth ; if his heart be throughly pierced by the Sword of the Law, still conscience calls upon him, and quarrells with him, and takes exceptions against him in the best of his duties, so farre they are from yeelding any satisfactiõ to God, or from bringing any peace to his conscience ; if hee rest upon the bare performance of them. I speake of a broken hearted sinner : for the conscience is now Eagle eyed, it was full of filme, and scales before, but now it is open and Eagle eyed, and can spy all his weakenesses, and picke matter of disquiet, even in the best of all his duties that are done.   The Soule thought them very good payment, yet now the heart is touched, and conscience is awakened, and tels him of his barrennesse, and deadnesse, and roaving thoughts, when he doth pray, and how insufficient he is to pray, and therfore he dares not pray with his Family, and conscience saith to him, you have formerly contemned prayer : and now you cannot pray. And when the Soule comes into the congregation, there Conscience notes him, and when he goes home, Conscience saith thus unto him, how dead were you, and how unreverently did you attend to the Word, and how unwil-

'ing

ling was your heart to be in subjection to the Word,
thus Conscience becomes Gods Serjeant, and saith,
doft thou thinke that thefe prayers will fave thee;
Nay, they are rather a meanes to condemne thee, fo
heartleffe, fo cold, and fo dead hearted thou art in
them; and is this hearing fufficient to fave thee: Nay,
will not the Lord curfe thee for thy weake performance of thefe duties? Now the diftreffed Soule
comes to a ftand with it felfe, and hee feeth fo much
weakeneffe in his duties, that he almoft leaves off all,
faying: I had as good not goe to the Word at all, for
I profit not by it; and I had as good not pray at all,
as pray thus deadly, and untowardly: thus the Lord
drives the Soule out of himfelfe; and when Confcience thus picks quarreles with him, and faith; will
prayer, and hearing, and thefe duties fo meanely performed, fave you? Nay, may not God juftly confound you for them? It is admirable mercy that God
did not confound you in hearing, and ftrike you dead
in praying! and then Confcience calls him in queſtion for his old finnes, and faith; if God may condemne thee for thefe duties, and for thefe prayers?
Then what may God doe for thy old drunkenneffe,
and railing at good men, and good meanes? as the A-
poftle faith, *If confcience condemne us; God is greater* 1 Ioh 3.20.
than our Confciences, and knoweth all things: fo the
Soule faith, I know thus much by my felfe, but God
knowes more.

    Thirdly, as the guilt of finne cannot be removed,   3.
nor Confcience quieted, meerely in the performance
of duties, if the Confcience be truely inlightened: fo
in the laft place, the fin that hath taken poffeffion in

the heart cannot be subdued by the power of any performance that he doth. I speake still of one that is not yet ingrafted into Christ : rebell against his sinne he will ; but kill it, and subdue it, that he cannot : and hence it is, that the Lord lets in upon the Soule a great many infirmities, and a swarme of weakenesses that are present with the Soule : and so he seeth an utter inabilitie in himselfe to help himselfe against them; the one of these two things befalls him. If he be a man of meane parts, and small gifts, he seeth himselfe so weake and so unprofitable under all meanes, that his Soule almost sinkes downe in desperate discouragement; and when he gets nothing by all the duties that hee doth, he falls out with himselfe, and pineth almost to desperation. And if he be a man of great parts and gifts, and learning, and hath wisedome to conceive of things ; the Lord suffers many corruptions to fall upon him : and when he comes to humble himselfe before God, he saith, I am able to discourse of this, and that ; and I can heare, and pray; but (oh) this heart of mine : a man had as good move a mountaine, as move my heart ; this hard heart will not stir, nor be broken under all, and helped against these as it should be. Now the Soule upon these termes is even content to leave off all : and it befalls the heart in this Gen. 11.15,16 case, as it did *Hager :* When her bottle of water was spent, she cast the child under a tree, and sat a far off, because she would not see the child die; so it is with the soule. When the bottles of these Saints, and scantie duties are done, the Soule sits downe in discouragement, and saith, Good Lord, it will never be, my Soule shall never be accepted, and my sins will never be be pardoned; and the heart begins to reafon thus with himfelfe, and faith; I have had as good meanes as ever any poore creature had, and many gracious friends have counfelled mee, and yet the guilt of my finnes is ever before mine eies; and my Confcience is not yet quieted : Nay, thefe finnes, this blind minde, and this hard heart will not be fubdued; but the Lord Iefus Chrift can doe more than thou, and the world too. The Lord will make thee fee that thou and the world can doe nothing, that Chrift may take away the guilt of fin, and quiet thy Confcience, and fubdue thy corruptions for thee : thus much he feeth from his owne experience.

The fecond paffage is this; as his owne experience makes the Soule confeffe that there is no hope of good in himfelfe; fo the example of others doth confirme a broken hearted finner in this; that all the creatures in the world, and all the duties under Heaven without Chrift, cannot purchafe falvation to the Soule; becaufe the Soule now feeth, and confiders in the Scriptures, that many thoufands have had all thefe priviledges, and done many duties, and yet come fhort of perfection. Many reprobates have had thefe priviledges as well as Gods people; and the Soule thinks thus with it felfe: If beautie, or honours, or riches, might have purchafed eternall life, then *Pharaoh, Abfolon,* and *Nebuchadnezzar,* fhould have beene accepted of God : therefore, What have I that many thoufands have not had? and, What doe I that reprobates have not done, and yet for ought I know, it never did them good? *Ifaac* was circumcifed, and fo was *Ifhmael* too; *Abel* offered Sacrifice, fo did *Caine*

too; and the ſtony ground receive the Word with
joy; and many there were that waited upon God in
the uſe of his Ordinances, as you may ſee in the Prophet *Eſay. Ahab* faſted, and *Iudas* repented, and yet he
is a devill now in hell this day: And the Prophet *David* ſaith, If the Lord ſhould marke what is done a-
miſſe, who could abide it? there was enough in *Da-
vids* prayers to condemne him; and if all theſe did
thus, and much more than I can doe; Then why
ſhould I think to find more helpe in my prayers then
they did: thus the ſoule ſeeth that Gods people never had Juſtification from any priviledges that they
enjoyed, nor from any duties that they did, without
relying on Chriſt.

Thirdly, the greatneſſe of the evill which now the
Soule ſeeth, and the deſperate miſery wherein it is, is
ſo great, that now it finds an utter in-abilitie, that all
the creatures under heaven ſhould ever remove the e-
vill of it. For the ſoare that is made, and the wound
that is given by ſinne, is broader than all the ſalve (that
the creatures can apply) is able to cover. The Word,
Sacraments, Prayer, and duties cannot reach the e-
vill that lies upon the heart in this particular; and
this is conſiderable; the meanes that muſt comfort
and quiet the heart in diſtreſſe muſt be able to beare
the wrath of God, and to take away the venome and
poyſon of the wrath of the Almightie. Now, the
Soule ſeeth that no creature can doe this; no creature
can beate backe Gods wrath but it will fall; and
hence it is that the Lord ſaith, hee hath laid ſalvation
upon one that is mighty; there are mighty corruptions, and mightie indignation, and mighty guilt, and
                                              therefore

therefore the Lord hath laid falvation upon the mightie. It muſt be more than a creature, that muſt beare or remove the wrath of the Creator; as the Text faith, *There is no other name under heaven, whereby you can be faved but onely by Chriſt,* Prayer faith, there is no falvation in me; and the Sacraments and Faſting fay, there is no falvation in us; there is falvation in no other but in Chriſt. The other are ſubſervient helps, not abſolute cauſes of falvation; as the holy Prophet *Ieremy,* ſhewing the peoples deſperate con- Ier.3.23. dition and their miſery therein, faith, *In vaine is ſalvation hoped for from the mountaines*; hee had ſaid be-fore in the 22 verſe, *Returne againe, oh diſobedient chil-dren and I will heale your rebellions,* and they anſwered, *Behold mee come Lord, for thou art the Lord our God, and in vaine is ſalvation hoped for from the mountaines*: By falvation in the mountaines is meant the Idols ſet up in the hills, which the poore people worſhipped, and thought they were able to ſuccour them, but in the day of trouble, they ſaid, we come Lord, for in vaine is falvation hoped for from the mountaines. So, if thou truſt in thy praying, and hearing, and good works, though thou hadſt a mountaine of them, they can doe thee no good, unleſſe with the eye of faith, thou lookeſt upon Chriſt for acceptance: but in the Lord our God is falvation for evermore. Then ga-ther up all: if the Soule ſeeth by experience, that no good will come by theſe, and if examples ſhew ſo much, and if the greatneſſe of the evill, ſhew that it is impoſſible for any comfort or pardon to be brought home to the ſoule; barely by theſe meanes, then the heart concludes thus, and ſaith; theſe will not doe

the

the deed, I may have all thefe priviledges, and performe all thefe duties, and yet falvation is not in thefe;
if I traft in them, there is no pardon in them, and no
hope of redemption from them faith the Soule. The
Soule doth not defpaire of all good in Chrift, but the
Lord is compeld (as I may fay with reverence) to
weary us from this confidence in our felves, and from
feeking any fuccour from our felves, that hee may
make us goe to Chrift.

Vfe 1.   This is a word of Exhortation. You fee that a
poore Soule finds nothing, and he hopes for no faving
fuccour from any meanes enjoyed, or duties performed, therefore wee ought to have our defires quickned, that fince we fee the way, and the duty required,
we muft not reft upon any thing here below. Since
our hearts muft be brought to this, and wee muft not
reft upon the bare performance of holy duties,
(though I doe not difhonour thefe duties, but onely
fpeake againft refting upon them) Oh, therefore
ftrive to come unto this, it will make you ready for
the riches of Gods mercy and goodneffe in Chrift
Iefus. Let us have our hearts raifed up from our own
bottoms, and let us plucke downe the foundations
that we have had in priviledges, or any fervice done
by us at any time. This is that which above all things
we muft doe; all the Saints of God have found this,
from day to day, after fearch made, then why fhould
we feeke for fuccour from thefe ; I fay, we muft not
neglect thefe duties, but we muft not reft upon them.
Be perfwaded to plucke off the handle of hope, from
of any thing that we doe, or any priviledge that God
gives us. Let us doe what we may, but yet goe be-
                                                    yond

yond all that we can do in this cafe; when your hearts are hankering after thefe crazie holds, ftay them, and deale by your hearts, as the Lord fometimes did with the people of *Iudea.* In their diftreffe, they did not goe to the Lord, but they went to *Egypt*, and *Nilus*, and therefore the Lord faid unto them : *What* Ier. 2 18. *haft thou to doe in the way of Egypt, to drinke downe the waters of Nilus? &c.* When they were thus ranging for their owne reliefe in the time of their trouble, the Lord (as it were) calls after them, and faith, you will downe to Egypt ? What have you to doe there ? Deale fo by your owne Soules, when thou findeft thine heart hammering helpe from it felfe, and catch-ing it out of the fire, thou feeft thy fins, and art trou-bled ; and now to quiet all, thou wilt heare, and pray, and performe duties, and thus thou thinkeft to forge comfort out of thine owne fhop ; therefore call upon thine owne heart and fay : What haft thou to doe to reft upon thefe broken ftaves, upon thy praying, and hearing, and profeffing ; thefe, if not accompanied with faith in Chrifts merits; will lay thee in the duft, and if thou makeft gods of them, the Lord will plucke them away. *Iudas* prayed, and preached, and heard, and received the Sacraments too, and yet he is a devill in hell this day, and except thou have more than he had, thou wilt be no better than he was : and therefore thinke thus with thy felfe ; what have I to doe to ftand here in thefe duties ? I may be deluded by thefe, but faved and comforted by them I cannot be, therefore ufe thefe I will, but reft upon them I will not. If I could looke up to heaven, and fpeake to *Abraham*, and *Paul*, and *David* ; and fay, how were

you

you faved; they would all make anfwer, and fay, oh, away to the Lord Chriſt, it is he that faved us, or elſe we had never come here; and he will fave you too, if you flie to him. Therefore (brethren) bring backe your hearts from theſe, and dreame not to receive any faving fuccour from what you have, or what you doe unleſſe you relie on Chriſt.

Queſtion.

But, me thinkes I heare fome fay; Oh, it is marvellous difficult, and hard; wee hang upon every hedge, and we are ready to thinke that it is enough, if we can but take up a taske in holy duties; how ſhall we plucke our hearts from reſting upon them?

For the anfwer to this queſtion; ſuffer mee to anfwer two things. Firſt, I will ſhew the meanes whereby we may finde all theſe hopeleſſe, and helpeleſſe reſting upon them. Secondly, I will ſhew when theſe meanes drive the heart truely to defpaire of all fuccour in them.

Anfwer.

Now, that we may finde theſe meanes to be fo to us, as they are in themſelves, and that our foules may be able to fay, It is true; theſe are the holy Ordinances of God, but it is in vaine to expect any falvation, or juſtification from them alone. I fay, the meanes are mainely foure, and I will handle them fomething largely; becauſe, if I be not deceived, here is the maine fett of a Chriſtian; and herein appeares the roote of old *Adam*; we will not part with our felves: the meanes are foure.

Firſt, confider ferioufly with thy felfe, and be convictingly fetled, and perſwaded, of the unconceiveable wretchedneſſe of thy naturall condition. If thou canſt but fee this throughly, it will make thee fee

how

how vaine it is to look for any fuccour from thy felf;
labour to fee the depth of thine owne mifery becaufe
of thy fin, and to fee how thou haft funk thy felfe into fuch a defperate gulfe of mifery; that all the means
under heaven will be fhort to fuccour thee, unleffe
the Lord Iefus come downe from heaven, and his infinite power be let down, to pluck up thy Soule from
that mifery wherein thou art: there thou lyeft, and
there thou art like to perifh for ever, if God in mercy
fuccour thee not. Now, that I may pull downe the
pride of every vile wretch, give me leave to difcover
the depth of our mifery, in thefe foure degrees.

First, confider that by nature thou art wholly deprived of all that abilitie, which God formerly gave
thee to performe fervice. *Whatfoever is borne of the
flefh is flefh:* (faith our Saviour) and therefore the A-
poftle *Paul* faith, *I know that in me, that is, in my flefh,
dwels no good thing.* All men by nature are flefh, and
therefore thinke thus with thy felf, and fay, there was
never good thought in my heart, nor good action
done by me, for in me dwels no fpirituall good thing:
there may be morall good in us, but though we are
good morally, yet we are nought fpiritually; howfoever you pranke up your felves, and thinke your
felves fome body, yet there is no fpirituall good in
you : unleffe God worke upon your hearts ; whatfoever you have thought, or done, is all in vaine.

Secondly, thou art not onely deprived of all fpirituall abilitie, but thou art dead in trefpaffes and fins.
What is that? a man is wholly poffeffed with a body
of corruption, and the Spawne of all abomination
hath overfpread the whole man, and it leavens all the

E whole

Foure degrees
of our mifery
by nature.

Ioh 3.6.
Rom 7.18.

2.
Degree of our
mifery.
Ephef. 2.1.

whole lumpe of body and minde. You often read this
phrafe in Scripture, but you perceive it not ; as it is
with a dead body being deprived of the foule (which
did quicken ir, and enable it to doe the workes of a
reafonable man) there comes a kind of fenfelefneffe,
and after that, all noyfome humours breed in the body; and all filthy vermine come from the body, and
therefore a man may bury it, but he cannot quicken
it any more. Juft fo it is with the Soule that is deprived of the glorious prefence of Gods Spirit, and grace
which *Adam* had in his innocency : For, looke what
the Soule is to the body, the fame is the grace of
Gods Spirit to the Soule. When the Soule is deprived of Gods Spirit, there followes a fenfeleffe ftupid-
neffe upon the heart of a man ; and all noyfome lufts
abound in the Soule, and take poffeffion of it, and rule
in it, and are fed there ; and appeare in a mans courfe
in this kind. There is no carrion in a ditch fmels more
loathfomely in the noftrils of man, than a naturall
mans workes doe in the noftrills of the Almightie:
There are fome workes of a dead body ; it rots, and
ftinkes, and confumes : fo, all the works of a naturall
man are dead workes: nay, all the *prayers of the wicked*
are an abhomination to the Lord. If you can but fay o-
ver the Lords Prayer, you thinke you doe a great
piece of worke ; but though thefe are good in themfelves, yet becaufe they come from a corrupt heart,
they are dead, and loathfome prayers in the noftrils
of the Almighty; as the wife man faith, *He that tur-*
neth his eare from hearing the Law, even his prayer is ab-
hominable. The prayers of a drunkard, of an adulte-
ter, or of a blafphemer, are an abhomination to the
                                        Lord ;

Prov. 28. 9.

Lord; He cannot abide them; they are such unsavorie, dead, stinking prayers, that the God of heaven abhors them : I would to God you were perswaded of it. I would have a man to reason thus with himselfe, and say; This is just my condition. How many gracious commands have I sleighted, and despised? How many precepts have I trodden under my feete; therefore even my best prayers are abhominable to the Lord; and if any prayers be such? then what is my person, and all my sinfull lusts? Looke what we doe with a dead body, wee may pitty him, and bury him, but we cannot quicken him : So we may pitty a poore drunkard, and pray for him, and bury him with teares; but we cannot save him : Nay, all the meanes in the world will not save him, except the Lords mightie power come from heaven to worke upon his heart.

Thirdly, the sentence of condemnation is now already past upon him, and one foot is in the pit already. *He that beleeves not, is condemned already* : He doth not say, he may be condemned; but the sentence is already past upon him : his hard heart was never soundly broken, and his proud heart was never content to part with it selfe, and all for Christ, and therefore he goes to endlesse torments for evermore. Every naturall man is an unbeleever, and therefore stands under the sentence of condemnation : So that, unlesse the Lord be pleased to open his eyes, and to breake his heart, and to draw him from that estate, he is like to perish, and goe to hell for ever.

Three degrees of our misery.

Iohn 3.18.

Fourthly, and lastly, if this be not enough, hee is not onely deprived of all spirituall good, and dead in

The fourth degree of our misery.

E 2   sinne,

sinne, and stands under the sentence of condemnation, though this were enough to lay our hearts low before the Lord. You see the sinner in the pit; But will you see him sinking into the bottome? I am loath to speake the worst: Nay, I durst not have thought it, had not the Lord Christ spoken it in his Word. Therefore see what he saith, *Have not I chosen you twelve, and one of you is a devill?* Who was that? It was *Iudas*. Why, what did he? What, a dead man, and a damned man, and a devill too: What will become of such a forlorne creature? It is said of *Iudas*, that the devill put it into his heart to betray Christ, out of a covetous humour to get money, and the *devill entred into Iudas.* Thus the devill puts it into his minde, and suggested it into his heart, to devise a way how to compasse his end: nay, the devill entred into *Iudas*, not by a corporall possession; but by a spirituall kinde of rule, which the devill did exercise over *Iudas*, that is, when the devills counsell, and advise took place with *Iudas* to betray his Master: this is not *Iudas* his condition alone, but it is the condition of all men by nature. That look as it is said of the Apostle, *They were inspired with the spirit of God*; and as it is said of all sound Christians, *They are led by the Spirit of God:* So, on the contrary, the wicked are led by, and with the spirit of the devill, *Hee that rules in the hearts of the children of disobedience:* The devill casts wicked thoughts into their hearts, and carries them into the commission of those evils, which formerly he had suggested: The devill rules in them; he speaks by their tongues, and workes by their hands, and thinkes, and desires, by their mindes, and walkes by their

Ioh. 6. 70.

Ioh. 13. 27.

Act. 1. 4.

Ephes. 2. 2.

their feete ; *The deuill shall cast some of you in prison,* Revel. 2. 10. saith S. *Iohn.* All men are naturally under the power of Sathan, and therefore Saint *Paul was sent to preach the Gospell, that hee might deliver him from the power of* Acts 26. 18. *Sathan to God.* You thinke your selues brave men, and you can despise the Word, and the grace of God, and abuse his Ministers : Alas, the devill hath power over you; as it is with a dead sheepe, all the carrion Crowes in the Countrey come to prey upon it, and all base vermin breed and creepe there : So it is with every poore naturall carnall creature under heaven; a company of devills, like so many carrion Crowes prey upon the heart of a poore creature, and all base lusts crall, and feede, and are maintained in such a wretched heart. Now (brethren) thinke of all these, and search seriously. It is better to know this now, than to know it when there is no remedy : I say no more for pittie; is it so with thee, and me, and all of us by nature? Then judge the case clearely, and passe the verdict. Dost thou thinke that a few faint prayers, and lazy wishes, and a little horror of heart can plucke a dead man from the grave of his sinnes, and a damned soule from the pit of hell, and change the nature of a devill to be a Saint ? No, it is not possible; and know that the work of renovation, is greater than the worke of thy creation, and there is no helpe in earth, either goe to Christ, or there is no succour for thee. We can pitty poore drunkards, and sorrow for them; but we are as able to make worlds, and to pull hell in pieces; as to pull a poore Soule from the paw of the devill. Nay, hee is a devill, and a damned devill, as you have heard : If this were well considered ; it would dash in pieces, all those carnall conceits of a great many, which make nothing of turning a devill to be a Saint.

The second meanes.

Secondly, consider seriously the infirmitie, and feeblenesse, and the emptinesse of all meanes that we enjoy, and all duties that we doe : it were argument enough, to perswade a poore broken-hearted sinner, not to relye upon a poore broken reed that will deceive him when he hath most neede : therefore since they cannot succour us, let us draw our hearts from resting on them. This is a matter of great weight also ; for the Soule being thus broken for sinne, sets a great matter of excellency, and sufficiency in holy duties. Nay, people hang all their hope of eternall life upon what they have, and what they can doe. Come to a poore broken-hearted sinner, and tell him of his sinne, that he stands guiltie of: Marke what his reply is, I confesse (saith he) it is true ; I have beene so, and so, but the world is well amended, I meddle not with my sinnes, and I have reformed all those base courses. Nay, the Lord knowes that my corruptions have cost me hot water, my heart hath beene exceedingly vexed with them, I hope, I have had my hell here, and I shall have no hell hereafter. Alas, poore wretch, is this the hope that upholds thy heart, and is this all the ground that thou goest upon? it is good that thou dost repent and amend, and reforme thy wayes, and blessed be God, for what hee hath made thee able to doe; but, this I must tell thee; If thy repentance, and reformation be all thy hope, and thou relyest upon them, as the Iewes did upon their Legall righteousnesse : thy Soule and all will sinke ever-

lastingly ,

laftingly; if thou look no further for help, for all thefe cannot procure thy acceptance before God in that great Day of accounts ; nor give any fatisfaction to Gods Juftice. Now the weakeneffe of all thefe priviledges and duties, may appeare in five particulars.

Firft, Thou canft not do that which God requires of thee, in all this that thou fo much braggeft of. *Thou* Rom. 8. 14. *haft a hard heart and canft not repent*: If thou canft doe what God requires of thee; then why doeft thou not break that hard heart of thine. It is a heart that cannot repent. The Saints of God find this; though they fee their fins, yet their hearts will not breake. Thou art as able to rend the rocks in pieces, as to breake thy hard heart. *The good that I would doe (* faith S. Paul) Rom. 2. 5. *I cannot doe, and the evill that I would not doe, that I doe.* The Church complaines of it, and faith, Why are our hearts hardened from thy feare ? Therefore **God** may juftly take exception againft thee.

Secondly, Thou art not many times carefull to do what thou canft; fometimes thou letteft paffe opportunities; and if thou takeft the occafions, it is marvellous flightly, and hoverly ; though God have put power and ability into thy heart, to performe holy duties ; fo, that thou feeft the occafions, yet thou flighteft them over moft fhamefully. *In many things* Iames 3. 2. *we fin all,* (faith the Apoftle S. *Iames*) and the Prophet *Efay* faith, *There is none that calleth upon thy name, nei-* Efay 64. 7. *ther ftirreth hee up himfelfe to take hold of thee.* It was the common fault of the wife Virgins, *they all flum-* Math. 25. 5. *bred:* this befalls even thofe that are the moft beloved of the Lord

Thirdly, Do what thou canft in the beft of all thy
fervices;

services; when thou commest to the highest pitch of the holinesse of thy heart, and to the most ferventest prayers that ever thou didst make, and the most broken heart that ever thou haddest, and the most exactest way of godlinesse; I say in the very best of all thy duties; there is still some imperfection, and for which God may in exact rigour frowne upon thee: now judge this; can that service save thee in which there is enough to condemne thee? thats impossible; in the best of thy duties there is enough to make God frowne upon thee. And therefore the Priest that was to offer Sacrifice; *Was to offer sacrifice for the sinne of his offering.* Where we see that even the holiest service that ever the Minister puts up to God, and in the best care that ever he exprest, he hath neede to offer Sacrifice for his offering: and so it is in all your services. You little thinke that God may condemne you, for your Prayers, and Sacraments, and Fastings. But I will make it cleare to you: for this is a common rule, we all beleeve in part, we know in part, and we love in part, so that, though our hearts are renewed, yet they are but renewed in part, there is some hatred mixed with our love, some unbeleefe with our faith, and some ignorance with our knowledge: And as the Apostle saith, *The flesh lusteth against the spirit, and the spirit against the flesh, so that these two are contrary the one to the other.* There is so much corruption in thee, so that when thou wouldest doe good, thou canst not doe it with that readinesse that thou oughtest; thou canst not doe it with all the whole streame of thy heart. The Law requires, that wee should love the Lord with all our hearts, and with all

our

Heb.7.27.

Gal.5.17.

our ſtrength ; So that we have no hangings backe in our duties ; but in allour prayers, and hearings, and readings, there is fleſh that oppoſeth the ſpirit, and corruption that croſſeth the worke of grace. So that we are not able to performe any ſervice, as God doth require of us: how backward are we to duties, and how weary in duties ? what wandring thoughts ? what privie pride ? and what ſeeking of our ſelves have we in them ? You know nothing, if you know not this ; but whether you know it or no, it is ſo. There is much corruption, oppoſing and thwarting the worke of the Spirit ; and therefore you had need pray for the repentance of your repentance ; and to beg the pardon of all your prayers : and whereas you thinke that you will repent, and amend, and heare, and pray, and the like ; I tell you, that though it be commendable to pray, and heare ; yet there is ſo much ſin in your amendment, and repentance, and duties ; that in exact juſtice God may curſe all that you doe, and execute his Judgement upon you for the ſame, therefore theſe cannot ſave you. Hee that heretofore hath prophaned the will, now ſanctifies it, and ſo he thinks all is quiet, but I tell thee that in all thy ſanctification of the ſame, thou haſt need of a Saviour.

Fourthly, where it is granted, and let it be ſuppoſed (which I confeſſe will not, nay can never be) but imagine it were ſo ; that after God hath opened a mans eies, and broken his heart, he ſhould never commit the leaſt ſin in all the world, and never have any failing in holy duties, nor any diſtemper in his Soule, though this cannot be ; but imagine it were ſo, that hee did never ſinne after his repentance, yet even the

F ſinne

finne of his nature which he brought in to the world
with him, were enough to make the Lord take the advantage of him for ever, and to caſt away all that e-
ver he doth as abominable from his preſence. Our
repentance, and our exacteſt performance of duties,
though we could doe them even to the uttermoſt: it
is a dutie that we are bound to doe, and the doing of
that which we owe ; can never ſatisfie for that which
hath beene done amiſſe by us: but our repentance of
ſinne, and our reformation, is a dutie which the Goſpell requires, and therefore will not ſatisfie for that
which is done amiſſe before our converſion. As a
Tennant that is run behind hand with his Land-lord
ſo many hundreths, and at laſt he begins to conſider
with himſelfe what he hath done, and he brings the
rent of the laſt halfe yeare when his leaſe is out ; will
this man thinke that he hath now ſatisfied his Land-
lord ? If hee ſhould ſay, now Land-lord, I hope you
are contented, and all is anſwered & I have fully paid
all that is betweene you and mee, you Land-lords
would be ready to reply thus, and ſay, This ſatisfies
me for the laſt halfe yeare paſt, but who payes for
the odde hundreds : ſo it is with a poore ſoule, be it
ſo, that after thoſe arrerages that thou haſt run upon
the ſcore with God, after all thy contempt, and pride,
and all thy Stubborneſſe of ſpirit, at laſt God opens
thine eyes, and breakes thy heart, and gives thee a ſight
of, and ſorrow for theſe ſinnes ; wilt thou come before the Lord, and ſay, Lord, I have repented of my
ſinnes paſt, and ſo I hope thy Juſtice is ſatisfied, and
all accounts made even betweene thee and me, the
Lord would anſwer, it is true thou doſt repent and
reforme

reforme thy selfe, the Gospell requires it, but who
payes the odde thousands, and who satisfies for thy
old drunkennesse, and for thy thousands of pride and
Stubbornesse, and all thy carelesnes, and all thy contempt of God and his grace, and who satisfies for all
thy blasphemies, and omissions of holy duties, and
the like, the Lord may justly take the forfeit of thy
Soule, and proceed in Judgement against thee to thy
destruction for ever. Our repentance and amendment
is a new dutie which the Lord requires of us from
the Gospell, but it is not the paying of the old debt;
for if we doe not repent, we stand guilty of the breach
of the Gospell, and so must satisfie for that sinne. The
breach of the Law is sinne, and the wages of sinne is
death, the wages of sin is not repentance nor amendment, but it is death: then repentance will not satisfie
for sinne : no, no, the wages that must be laid downe
for a mans sin, is death. As the Lord said, *In the day* Gen. 2. 17.
that thou eatest of the forbidden fruit, thou shalt die the
death. And therefore the Apostle saith, cursed is every Gal. 3. 10.
one that continues not in all things written in the Law to
doe them. Repentance is onely a worke of the Gospell
to bring our hearts in frame againe, but the breach of
the Law must be satisfied for ; so that having sinned
against the Lord, and wronged his Justice, we must
either die our selves or have one to die for us ; then,
there is no laying downe of any satisfaction to God
by any thing that we can doe in this case, but we must
have recourse to our Saviour, who onely can satisfie
Gods wrath for our sinnes.

Fifthly, as a sinner is utterly unable to bring himselfe into a good estate, by all the meanes that he can

use; so he is unable to maintaine his lot: and to keepe himselfe aforehand in a Christian course, when he is brought unto it. Therefore as it is necessary to have a Saviour to pardon us : So, it is necessary to have a Saviour, to continue that estate of grace to us for our good. When the Lord in mercy had given to *Adam* in his innocency, perfect holinesse, and righteousnesse; insomuch, that hee was able to keepe the Law, and to purchase favour for himselfe, *Adam* then fell, and spent all that stocke of grace; and if we had our stocke in our own hands, we should spend all and be ruinated for ever, if God did leave us to our selves. If *Adam* having no sinne could not keepe himselfe in that happy estate; much lesse are we able that have much corruption in us; therefore it is not only required to go to Christ for grace to pardon us, but we must go to Christ to maintaine our grace, and to keepe our hearts in frame here, and to bring us to a Kingdome for ever hereafter. When *Adam* had spent all the stocke of grace; and proved a bankrupt, the Lord would raise him up againe; but he would not put the stocke into his hands againe; but he puts it into the hands of Christ. As a man that gives his child a portion, and he spends it all; now his father will raise him againe, but will not put it into his own hands, but into the hands of some friend, and will have his sonne goe to that man for his allowance every day, and for every meale : So, it is with the Lord our heavenly Father, because we have misspent all that wisdome and holinesse, and righteousnesse, which God gave *Adam*, and in him to all of us; therefore the Lord would not put the stock of grace

into.

into our own hands again, but he hath put it into the
hands of Chrift, and will have us depend upon Chrift
for every crum of grace; yea, even for the will to do
any good; we muft goe to him, that he may preferve
and maintaine the worke of grace in us; and wonderfull happy are we that it is fo. For, fhould the Lord
fet the devill and us together, all were gone. The
Lord Iefus gives grace, and continues it, and helpes
us to perfevere in grace; and fo makes us come to the
end of our hopes, even the falvation of our Soules.
Oh therefore, looke up to the Lord Iefus Chrift;
and fay, Oh it is a bleffed mercy; that when my
heart is proud, vaine, loose, and foolish; that then I
may goe to the Fountaine of grace, for humilitie, and
for grace. We are kept (faith Saint *Peter*) *By the power* 1 Pet. 1.5.
of God through faith unto falvation: As if hee had faid,
all the powers of hell and darkeneffe are come about
us, and a world of wickedneffe befets us, and all the
powers of the world, and the corruptions of our own
hearts allure us. Now, we cannot ftand by our owne
ftrength, therefore we have need of a Chrift, that we
may be kept by his power, and be able to fuffer, and
to do any thing for his Names fake, and that he may
preferve us in that great day of accounts. And the A-
poftle *Iohn* faith, *Little Children you are of God, and have* 1 Iohn 4.4.
overcome the world, for greater is he that is in you, than
he that is in the world. Hee doth not fay, greater are
you, than he that is in the world, but greater is hee
that is in you, &c. He doth not fay, greater is your
humilitie than your pride; greater is your patience,
than your impatience; and greater is your love, than
your hatred; but he faith. The Lord Iefus is greater

in

in us, to succour and to helpe us; then all the temptations of the devill, and the corruption of our hearts that can presse in upon us, to doe us any hurt, or to hinder us in a Christian course. Dost thou thinke thy owne hearing, and praying, and duties will serve the turne and save thy Soule? No, no, thou art an undone man, if thou rest upon thy owne crazie bottomes; Amend thou mayst, and pray thou oughtest; but these will not save thee; these will not cause the acceptation of thy person with God; nor justifie thy Soule before his Tribunall. All these are poore, weake, and crazie meanes. For if thou canst not doe what God requires; and if thou dost not what thou art able, and if in the best of thy services; there is pride, and stubbornnesse enough to condemne thee, and when thou risest up from prayer, thou hadst need pray againe for pardon of thy prayer: Nay, couldst thou doe all that thou shouldest after conversion; in the most strict and exactest manner; yet that doth not satisfie for the sin, that thou hads committed before conversion; and if thou canst not maintaine thy owne grace, then there is an absolute necessitie of going to Christ for all. Nay, aske your owne hearts, and services; and say thus: Prayer, wilt not thou save me? and Hearing, wilt not thou save me? they will all professe plainely, and say; salvation is not in me (saith Prayer) and salvation is not in mee (saith Hearing) and salvation is not in me (saith repentance, and amendment:) Indeed, we have heard of a Christ, that he hath died and satisfied, and suffered, and risen, and delivered his poore servants; and pluckt poore Soules from hell; and we need a Saviour to pardon us, alas, wee cannot save our selves. All thy duties will say to thee, as the King said to the woman, when the famine was great in Samaria: *And as the King was going upon the wall, there cried a woman to him, saying,* 2 King.6,25. *Helpe, oh King. And the King made this answer, If the* 27. *Lord God succour not, how can I helpe?* So, me thinkes the soule saith; when it is besieged with the wrath of God? Oh helpe prayer, and hearing, and Sacraments, and the like: Me thinkes I heare them reply in this matter; Alas, how can wee helpe, you have prayed sinfully; and heard the Word untowardly; and received the Sacraments unworthily? Oh, let us all goe to heaven for a Mediator; good Lord, pardon the sinne of these prayers, and these hearings, and the unworthinesse of these Sacraments; and all this frothinesse, and deadnesse in hearing: Thus they will all send you to heaven for a Christ; and say, alas, I cannot save you; how many commands have I disobeyed? how many duties have I sleighted, and therefore send to Christ for pardon; we are weake and feeble, and onely come to the eare, and to the eye; but the Lord Iesus must come downe from heaven, and be powerfull, every way to doe good to your Soules. You must goe to a Christ, to batter the proud flesh; and to pardon all that is amisse, and to performe all duties that you would have done. When *Elisha* tooke up the cloake of *Eliah,* he said, *where is the God of E-* 2 King 2.14 *liah?* he did not say, Where is the cloake, but where is the God of *Eliah.* All the ordinances of God, are but as the barke of the tree; but Christ and the Promise are the pith. The heart, and life, and power of all is in Christ onely: therefore looke higher then

these,

these, for they doe all proclaime; that there is no succour but in Christ.

The third meanes to drive our hearts from resting upon our duties is this. We must consider the unconceiveable hazzard, and danger, and the inconvenience that will come if we put any affiance in any of those priviledges that we have, or any duties that we performe. The very consideration hereof is able to withdraw our hearts from resting upon them. The danger appeares in two particulars.

First, the carnall confidence in what wee have, and doe; shut a man out from having any part in Christ. He that is guiltie of this sinne, withdrawes himselfe from the favour of the Lord: and hee becomes uncapable of that mercy & good which God hath revealed ; and Christ hath purchased for poore distressed sinners. For this is all that the Lord lookes for at our hands, that we should deny our selves, and wholly cast our selves upon his goodnes and mercy: nay, that man which relies upon what he doth, puts himself without the reach of all that mercy and great salvation that is in Iesus Christ. Christ came not to call the righteous to repentance, nor them that trust in themselves; nor them that thinke they can save themselves, but he came to call sinners to repentance, and those that see an utter insufficiency in themselves to save or succour themselves in the day of trouble, there is great salvation in Christ, and plenteous redemption purchased by Christ, and you heare of all this, and it is all true, but this I must tell you, all that Christ hath done and deserved, shall never doe you good, if you rest upon your selves. You doe thinke

that

that it is such a great sinne, as indeed it is, sometimes you make conscience of drunkennesse and other sins, if you make conscience of any thing, then know that this is the greatest sinne in the world. See how the A- Gal. 5. 2. postle sets himselfe against this carnall confidence, where speaking to the *Galathians* that trusted in their owne circumcision, that answers to our Baptisme : Behold (saith he) I *Paul*, say, I, not a bare man, but I *Paul* inspired with the Spirit in a extraordinary manner, and I, an Apostle that doe not, nay, that cannot erre, I that have received a commission from the Lord, I say, that if you be circumcised, that is, if you trust in your Circumsition, Christ shall profit you nothing : nay, (saith hee) *Iesus Christ is made of none* Verse 4. *effect to you, if you seeke to be justified by the workes of the Law.* If you rest in the merit of your prayer, Christ is made of none effect to you, and you shall never receive any power from the death of Christ : the blood of Christ will never purge those filthy hearts of yours, and his resurrection shall never quicken you. Whatsoever your case and condition is, or can be, if your sins were never so haynous for greatnesse, continuance, and for number, if you will but renounce your selves and go to Christ; nothing shall condemne you : but if your sins were reformed, if you trust in them, all your reformation, nay, Christ himselfe shall never doe you good. It is with the Soule of a poore sinner, as it is with the body of a man. If it had some slightie disease or sicknes, and that may (haply) be cured, but if his throate begin to swell, and the vitall passages be stopped up that he can receive no meate, nor physicke, every neighbour will say, he is but a

G   dead

dead man, all the meanes and men in the world can doe him no good, he can receive nothing downe : So it is with the Soule ; it is annoyed with many base corruptions, and sinfull distempers ; and if it be wounded with many rebellions ; there is meanes enough in Christ to cure all? If thou be a filthy besotted drunkard, or an adulterer, the blood of Christ can purge thy drunken adulterous heart, one touch of Christ can cure all thy bloody issue. If thou wert dead in trespasses and sinnes, the Lord Iesus could quicken thee, and raise thee from death to life; but if thy proud heart swell with thy owne sufficiencie, and thou wilt rest upon thy selfe, all the merits and grace in Christ can doe thee no good. This is the maine conclusion, into which all the rest is resolved. *You will not come to me* (saith our Saviour) *that hee might be saved.* He doth not say; you have many sins, and shall not be saved ; but, you will not come to me, &c. that is, you will not goe out from your selves to the Lord Christ; and therefore cannot receive mercy and grace from his Majesties hands : though thou art never so base and vile, if thou couldest goe to the Lord Iesus, and rest upon his mercy, nothing should stand betweene thee and heaven, but if thou stickest in thy self, all the grace in Christ can doe thee no good.

    Secondly, This carnall confidence, makes a man unprofitable under all the means that God bestowes; As the Prophet *Ieremy* saith, *Cursed is he that trustes in the arme of flesh, and departs from the Lord* ; Why ? What shall become of him? the text saith, *he shall be like an heath in the wildernesse, and shall never see good.* The nature of the heath is this; though all the dew of

Ioh. 5. 40.

Ier.7.5,6.

heaven

heaven, and all the showers in the world fall upon it; and though the Sunne shine never so hotly, it will never grow fruitfull, it will never yeeld any fruit of increase, but it is unfruitfull still. Such a Soule thou wilt be; thou that resteth upon thy owne services, and sayest; because thou hearest, and prayest, and doest sanctifie the Lords Day; therefore thou must needs goe to heaven; I say, thou shalt never see good by all the means of grace; if thou makest them independant causes of salvation; all the promises in the Gospel shall never establish thee, and all the judgements in the world will never terrifie thee; thou shalt never have any saving grace wrought in thee by them: The truth is, he that hath all meanes, and hath not a Christ in all; he shall never see good by all. Therefore thou that restest upon thy parts, and gifts, and upon thy duties; thou wilt have a heart so besotted, that grace will never come into thy heart, and God will never quiet thy conscience. It may be a poore drunkard is converted and humbled; but thou standest still, and canst get no good by all the meanes in the world. Therefore say thus to thy selfe: doth this carnall confidence cut me off from all the grace and mercy that is in Christ; and without mercy, and pardon from Christ I am undone for ever; and without grace I am a poore defiled wretch here, and shall be damned for ever after; if I rest here, I may bid adue to all mercy: Nay, all the meanes that I have, will never do me good. Is this the fruit of my carnall confidence? Oh Lord withdraw my heart from it.

Lastly, when all the meanes of grace, will not The four plucke away the Soule from resting upon it selfe, meanes,

when reason will not rule him, nor meanes will not
prevaile with a poore sinner, as commonly a great
while they will not, then the Lord tires a poore
Soule with his owne distempers. And the Lord
deales with the Soule, as an enemie deales with a
Castle that hee hath besieged; when the Citizens
will not yeeld up the Castle, he famisheth them, and
cuts off all provision, and makes them consume within, and so at last they are forced to resigne it up upon
any termes. So, when the Lord hath laid siege to a
carnall heart, and hath shewed him his wofull condition, and yet the heart will not off, nor will not take
up any tearmes of peace, but stil he will shift for himselfe. Now, what doth the Lord doe? he takes away
the comfort of all the meanes that he hath, till hee is
famished with the want of Gods favour; and then he
is content to yeeld up all to the God of heaven and
earth. It was just so with this Prodigall; all the world
could not perswade him but hee might live better of
his portion, and so away he goes; and when hee had
tried the world, and could get no succour, at last hee
confest, it was better to be at a fathers finding, & now
he saw that a fathers house was admirably good, and
that the servants and children in their fathers house
are happy; for they have bread enough, and enough
againe, and to spare too: and so he is forced to return.
So, it is with many poore distressed soules: all the
arguments under heaven cannot quiet them, and all
the meanes in the world cannot plucke them from
themselves; and wee tell them daily, that they must
not expect grace, nor power, nor pardon from themselves; *It is mercy and peace* (saith the Apostle. You
would

aIohn 3.

would have peace of conscience, and pardon of sinne,
and assurance of Gods love; and whence would you
have it, you would have it from your duties? it is not
prayer and peace, nor hearing, and peace; but it is
mercy and peace; and therefore away to the Lord
Jesus, that you may receive a mercy from him: Yet we
cannot get poore creatures from themselves, but they
would faine shuffle for themselves, and have a little
comfort of their owne, and they say, Lord, cannot my
prayers, my care and fasting merit salvation? Now,
what doth God then? he saith to such a Soule, goe
try thy, put to then best of the strength, and use all
the meanes that thou canst, and see what thou canst
doe; See if thou canst cure thy conscience, and heale
those wounds of thine; and suddue the corruptions
of thy heart, with thy prayers and abilities: but when
the Soule hath made triall, and weltred, and wearied it selfe, at last, he finds that all the meanes he can
use cannot quiet him, nor comfort his conscience, and
the poore sinner is pinched and wearied, and the
Lord will not answer his prayers, nor sweeten the
desires of his Soule, and the Lord will not blesse the
Word to him for his comfort, and at last, the Soule
saith: Such a poore Christian (even a man of meane
parts, and weake gifts) how is hee comforted, and
such a prophane drunkard is puld home, & hath gotten the assurance of Gods love; the Lord hath puld
downe the proud hearts of such and such; and they
live comfortably, and sweetly; and I have no peace
nor assurance of Gods love. You may thanke your
selves for it; they saw nothing, and they looked for
nothing from themselves; and therefore they went

home to the gate of mercy to the Lord Jesus Christ, and they have bread enough, if you would come home to Christ, you might have beene comforted also. Now therefore go to the Lord Iesus Christ, and as certainly as God is in heaven; refreshing and comfort will come into your hearts, and mercy (which is better than marrow) shall satisfie those feeble fainting spirits of yours. You see what the way is, and what the helps be to plucke off our hearts from resting upon these duties, and therefore thinke thus with thy selfe, and say, is my misery so great ? are my duties so weake? and is my carnall confidence so dangerous ; that I may be troubled for ever ? for any thing that I can doe for my selfe ; and is comfort no where else to be had, but in the Lord Iesus Christ ? Oh then Lord, work my heart to this dutie. Stick not in your selves to doe all this, but goe beyond all that you can doe, and labour so to approve your hearts to God, that you may see greater mercy in God, than all that you can doe.

Now there are two Cavils, which carnall persons slander this truth of God with all; and these must be answered before I can come to the trials.

The first cavill with which wretches are content upon this truth, it is this. Oh say they ? What, is it so, that all our prayers, and hearings, all our care, and desires, and all our improvement of meanes are nothing worth? will not all these justifie us ? nor make us exceptable to God? then let us cast care away, let us sweare, and ryot, and drinke, and live as we list, we heare that all the duties that we can doe, will not save us, the Minister tells us so. Thus a company of carnall

nall wretches runne headlong downe to eternall deſtruction, one ſweares, and another caſts all the commandements of God behind his backe.

To this I anſwer. Doth the Miniſter ſay ſo; nay, *Anſwer,*
the Word, the Scripture, the Spirit of God ſaith ſo,
and the Lord Ieſus himſelfe ſpeakes it. In the meane
time wilt thou gaine-ſay that which the Lord Chriſt
hath ſpoken? Doth not the Apoſtle ſay. *You are ſa-*
ved not of workes, &c. And in another place, *It is not in* Rom.9.16.
him that wills, nor in him that runs, but in the Lord that
ſhewes mercy. It is the Spirit of God that ſaith it, and
doſt thou ſtand to out-face the Lord Jeſus Chriſt in
it? But ſtay a while, and take a full anſwer with thee,
and know theſe three things, thou that doſt abuſe this
doctrine of Gods free favour. Firſt, howſoever thy
good workes are not ſufficient to ſave thee, yet thy e-
vill workes are enough to damne thee. As the Apo-
ſtle ſaith, *that all they might be damned which beleeved* 2 Theſ.2.12.
not the truth but had pleaſure in unrighteouſneſſe. You
that take pleaſure in your drunkenneſſe, and prophanneſſe, and in your gibing and jeſting at the meanes of
grace, there is roome enough in hell for you all : that
all you might be damned. Yea, thou that delighteſt
in thy drunkenneſſe, thou maiſt drinke down thy laſt,
and thy damnation too, and thou that blaſphemeſt a-
gainſt the truth of Chriſt, take heed that God power
not downe his wrath upon thee. It is true, though thy
good workes are not perfectly good and cannot ſave
thee, yet thy bad workes are perfectly naught and
will condemne thee: nay, thy prayers are an abomination to the Lord, and will the Lord ſave thee for
that which is abominable to him? thou thinkeſt
hell

hell is broke loofe, becaufe mercy is come into the world, this thy wickedneffe will condemne thee for evermore. Secondly, they that thus ftand it out a- gainft Gods free grace in Iefus Chrift (the Lord in mercy open their eyes, my Soule mournes for them and for that ftrange punifhment that fhal befal them, except the Lord break their hearts in time) as any fin is enough to condemne them, fo their fin is of an un- conceiveable hainoufneffe, and their judgement will be anfwerable. Their finne is become out of meafure finfull, becaufe mercy is revealed, and they have made a mocke of it. The very height of all, that wrath that is in God fhall be their portion. Good Lord, is it pof- fible that ever any man fhould dare to defpife the mercy of God, and to trample the blood of Chrift under his feete, and not onely to commit wanton- neffe, but to turne the grace of God into wanton- neffe, and to make the Lord Chrift the Patron of their filthineffe ? How will the Lord Iefus take it at their hands : that, whereas the Lord Iefus came into the world to deftroy the works of the devill, they fhould make Chrift a meanes to uphold the workes of the devill. Oh, that ever any man fhould dare to finne, becaufe mercy abounds ! and becaufe they heare that Chrift will one day fave them, therefore they in the meane time will do all they can againft him that muft fave them. See what S. *Paul* faith againft fuch, *Defpi- feft thou the riches of his goodneffe, long fufferance and forbearance, not knowing that the goodneffe of God lea- doth to repentance, but after thy hardneffe of heart, thou treafureft up to thy felfe wrath againft the day of wrath.* Thou that liveft in the bofome of the Church, where the Angels come downe from heaven, and rejoyce in

Rom. 2. 4, 5.

in this free grace of God in Chriſt, and haſt thou the
offer of this mercy, and doeſt thou deſpiſe it? then thy
drunkenneſſe is not bare drunkenneſſe, but there is a
treaſure of vengeance in it. And thou ſayeſt, thou
wilt be drunke, and prophane, becauſe thy ſobrietie
and the good workes cannot ſave thee. I tell thee, it
is not bare ſcorning, and bare prophanneſſe, but there
is a maſſe of vengeance in all theſe. And when thou
ſhalt ſtand before the judgement ſeate of Chriſt, and
ſhall be indited for a drunkard, and a ſcorner, and a
prophane perſon, and ſuch a one as haſt toſſed the
people of God with ſcorners upon thy Ale-bench;
when the Law hath thus proceeded againſt thee, then
will mercie come in againſt thee, and ſay, Lord, execute vengeance upon him for me, and for me, ſaith a-
nother, for I have bin diſhonoured, and becauſe mercie did abound, he would have his ſinne abound alſo.
And then comes in the blood of Chriſt, and cryes a-
loud, ſaying, Vengeance againſt that drunkard, indeed
Lord, there's a poore wretch that knew no other, but
vengeance (Lord) againſt that drunkard, and that
ſcorner, becauſe my blood was ſhed, and mercy was
offered, and he deſpiſed it. You that know your drunken neighbours and ſervants, and ſee their rioting and
ſcorning, tell them that there is a treaſure of vengeance in thoſe ſins; and you that are guilty of it, goe
your wayes home and mourne, and the Lord give us
hearts to mourne for you. You that know what this
ſinne is, when you goe to the Lord in Prayer, put up
one petition for them, and ſay good Lord take away
that treaſure of vengeance. Oh, pray that if it be poſſible this great ſin may be pardoned. Thirdly, all ſuch

H   perſons

persons muſt know that it is carnall confidence, in the meanes that withdrawes a bleſſing from them in the uſe of the meanes. *what things were gaine to me* Phil. 3.7. (ſaith Saint *Paul*) *I accounted liſſe for Chriſt*; that is, when he put any confidence in them, he loſt the benefit of the meanes.

Secondly, Some will ſay, you doe nothing but re-The ſecond cavill. prove us for duties, and labor to pluck us from them: then why ſhould we pray, and heare, and what good ſhall we have by all that we do, if we cannot be ſaved by theſe meanes; then, what uſe is there of them?

Anſwer. To this I anſwere. Yes, there is great uſe of them, and much good to be had by them: As the Apoſtle Titus 3. 14. ſaith; *Let us alſo learne to maintaine good workes* for neceſſary uſes: when he had ſpoken of free Juſtification through his grace; then the Text ſaith, teach a man to maintaine good workes for neceſſary uſes: and in verſes 4 & 5. the 4. and 5. verſes, he ſaith; *After that the kindneſſe, and love of God our Saviour towards man, appeared not by workes of righteouſneſſe which we have done, but according to his mercie he ſaved us by the waſhing of regeneration.* Now, leaſt any man ſhould ſay, if God doe not ſave a man for his workes, then why ſhall we doe good workes and the like? See what he addes; Let us learne to maintaine good workes, &c. There are many neceſſary uſes of the meanes, though they be not meritorious, & of abſolute ſufficiency, Were not he a mad man that ſhould ſay, what ſhall I doe with my money if I cannot eate it? And what ſhall I doe with my boate if I may not dwell in it? A man may buy meate with his money, and row with his boate. So, you muſt uſe all meanes, and improve all impor-

tunities

tunities, and if ever pray and faſt, pray and faſt now
in theſe daies of trouble,but think not to be ſaved,nor
juſtified by the worth and merit of them : yet uſe
them for ſome neceſſary uſes;and the uſes are three. *Vſe.* 1.

First, We muſt uſe all the meanes that God gives *Of the meanes.*
us as guides,to leade us by the hand to the Lord Jeſus
Chriſt; and as lights to ſhew us where life is to bee
had. *Iohn Baptiſt* profeſſed plainely, that he was not
the Meſſiah, but he pointed at him, and ſayd, *Behold*
the Lambe of God that takes away the ſinnes of the world.
So,I ſay,all the ordinances of God which are honourable, and commendable,and comfortable; they all
profeſſe, that they are not our Saviours : onely they
point us to a Saviour,even the Lord Jeſus Chriſt;the
Word reveales Chriſt,and Prayer goes to a Chriſt,
and the Sacrament preſents Chriſt to us; and therefore they al ſay with one accord,let us go to the Lord
Jeſus, and looke up to him. When your hearts are
troubled and diſquieted, all your duties knocke at
your hearts,and ſay, would you not have mercie, and
power againſt corruption, and ſome evidence of
Gods favour? Oh (ſay you) it is that which we want,
and it is all that we deſire in this world; Come then
(ſaith Prayer and the Word) we will goe to Chriſt
with you; there is all fulneſſe in him : this is the end
of all the holy ordinances of God,not to make them
Saviours, but to lead us to a Saviour.

Secondly,as they are guides to leade us to a Chriſt, *Vſe.* 2.
ſo they are meanes to convey grace, mercy and com- *Of the meanes.*
fort from Chriſt to our ſoules. Though they are not
meat,yet they are ẃ diſhes that bring the meat.They
are the meanes whereby ſalvation hath beene revea-

led

led, and is conveyed to you. There is a fountaine of grace in Chriſt, but the Word, and Prayer, and Sacraments, and Faſting, theſe are the conduits to convey this water of life, and to communicate this grace to us. You doe not uſe to drinke the conduit, but the water that the conduit brings. Aske, that your joy may be full, (ſaith our Saviour) and ſo the Lord ſpeakes by the Prophet *Eſay, Incline your eare, and come unto me, heare and your ſoules ſhall live.* As if he had ſayd, waite upon God in his Word and Ordinances, and your ſoules ſhall live. Though the meanes are not life it ſelfe, yet life is conveyed by them. *In Chriſt are hid all the treaſures of wiſedome and knowledge.* If you would have any grace and holineſſe, the treaſure of it is in Chriſt. The Word is as the Indenture or great Will of God whereby the treaſure of Gods favour is made knowne to your Soules. The bond or will is not the treaſure, but conveyes the treaſure to us, and makes us have a right, and title to it: our Saviour ſaith, *My peace I leave with you, my peace I give unto you,* and all the promiſes in Chriſt are, yea, and Amen: yea, that is truth it ſelfe, and, Amen, that is confirmed now, you muſt receive the tenure of all theſe in Chriſt. And the holy Sacraments, are as the broad ſeales whereby the Covenant of grace is confirmed, made authenticall and ratified to your Soules. When a man hath much goods and lands and would make another his heire, he paſſeth his lands or goods over to him by will, and if the will is not onely drawne but alſo ſealed, then, though this Will is not the treaſure it ſelfe, yet it is a ſpeciall meanes to convey this treaſure to the heire that muſt

have

Eſay 55. 3.

Colloſſ. 2. 3.

have it. So, the Word is the will of God, and the Sacraments are the Seales of it, and all that mercy and goodnesse in Christ is made knowne to you by the Word, and made sure to you by the Sacraments; the Word and Sacraments are not this treasure, but they are blessed meanes to convey this treasure to your Soules. Therefore, when your hearts are dead, weake, and heavie, and you begin to breath for some consolation, saying, who will tell me how I may have my dead heart quickned, and my heavy heart refreshed, as *David once breathed for the water of Bethlem*; then me thinkes the Word and Prayer, and Sacraments doe all say, we will goe to the Lord Jesus Christ for all these for you, and then Christ will sanctifie you in his Word, and if you have strong divels hanging upon you, fasting and prayer, will fetch power and grace from Christ; and cast all these devills out: So then you see their good use of all these.

Thirdly, the last use of the meanes is this, that by the exercise of our selves in them; and by the improvement of our times and meanes, we may glorifie the God of grace that hath given us all these meanes, and that we may waite upon him with feare and reverence, and honour God in his Word, and come to his Table, and there partake of the dainties of life and salvation, and expresse the vertues of him that hath called us to this marvellous light, that we may see Gods grace in prayer, and in professing, and delight in the duties of his worship. These are all very good uses; so then, the conclusion is this, you must not thinke that your duties can pardon one sinne, yet they must be used, and blesse God for them, and (if ever)

Vse. 3.
Of the meanes.

now

now is a time to improve all thefe, for they are a
meanes to leade us to Chrift, and to convey grace and
life from Chrift into our foules, and thereby we may
glorifie the God of grace that hath beene fo mercifull to us. The fecond thing that I mentioned is this.

When we doe defpaire of all helpe in the meanes.

When fhall we know that our hearts are brought to
this paffe, that the meanes of grace doe work fo kindly that our hearts may be brought to this holy defpaire? I would not have you goe away, and fay, the
Minifter faith, we muft defpaire. Its true, you muft
defpaire of all faving fuccour in your felves, but you
muft not defpaire of all mercy in Chrift.

Anfwer.

For the anfwere to this queftion you muft know
that there are three particular trialls of our owne
hearts, whereby we fhall know when the Lord is
pleafed to deale fo kindly and fweetely with us, as to
drive us from our felves to Chrift.

The firft triall.

Firft, the Soule of a poore finner that feeth all
meanes helpeleffe and hopeleffe in themfelves, will
freely confeffe and acknowledge (and that openly)
that the worke of falvation is of an unconceiveable
difficultie, and he feeth an utter infufficiencie and impoffibilitie in himfelf, and in any means in the world
to be faved of himfelf: He feeth that it is beyond his
power, and the ftaffe is out of his owne hand, and the
Soule almoft finkes under it, and conceives it almoft
impoffible to come out of it, in regard of that which
it apprehends. He feeth now that all thofe broken
reeds, and rotten props, and all that boldneffe whereby the heart did beare up it felfe, they are all broken
in pieces, and all thofe Caftles which he hath built in
the ayre, wherein hee comforted himfelfe with
dreames

dreames of confolation, they are all throwne downe
to the ground, and battered about his eares, and now
the Soule wonders how he was fo deluded, to truft
to fuch lying vanities, and to fuch deceitfull fha-
dowes. This is the difference that the foule will finde
in it felfe before this worke of converfion, and after
it is wrought. Before, a man thinkes it an eafie matter to come to heaven, and judgeth it a foolifhneffe in
people to be caft down and difcouraged in the hardneffe and difficultie of the worke of falvation; and he
conceives it to be a foolifh conceite in the franticke
braine of fome precife Minifters? Oh (faith he) God
bleffe us, if none be faved, but fuch as thefe, whatfoever he faith, a man may goe to heaven, and repent,
and get the pardon of his fins, it is nothing but con-
feffing his finnes before God, and craving mercy for
the pardon of them, and is this fuch a hard matter;
this man in the dayes of his vanitie, thinkes he hath
heaven in a ftring, and mercy at command, and hee
can come to heaven, and breake his heart at halfe an
houres warning: but take this man when the Lord
hath awakened his confcience, and put him to the triall; when he feeth that after all his prayer and teares,
yet his confcience is not quieted, and his finnes are
not pardoned, and the guilt ftill remaines, now he is
of another mind, now he wonders at himfelfe that he
was fo deluded, and now he faith, where is the deluded heart, that did thinke it, and the mouth that did
fpeake it? Nay, he thinkes it a great mercie of God,
that he is not in hell long agoe; and he ftands and
wonders that ever any man comes to heaven, and he
faith, certainely their hearts are not like mine; and
their

their sinnes are not so great as mine, good Lord, who can ever be saved such a divell to tempt, and such a world to allure, and such corruptions boyling within. He wonders how *Abraham* got to heaven beyond the Starres, and *Moses*, but above all *Manasses*; yet he saith, blessed be God that ever he did this for them, but for my selfe (all things considered) I think it a matter impossible, how I, nay, how can I ever be wrought upon? shall ever any mercie comfort me? and shall ever any meanes doe me good? Why have not all those meanes that I have had done me good, I shall never have power to pray better than I have done, and I shall never be able to wrestle with God more earnestly than I have done; and yet I see all meanes profit not; therefore I am but a gone man. I am but lost, and I know not which way my soule should be saved. When our Saviour Christ was discovering the difficultie of the way to Salvation; His Disciples sayd, *Good Lord, who then shall be saved?* So the poore soule saith; Oh the means that I have had, and the prayers that I have made; so that I have thought the heavens did even shake againe, and yet, Good Lord, my heart did never stirre at all, and therefore how can I be saved? And as the Prophet *Ieremy* saith, *Shame hath eaten up the labours of our fathers, and we lye downe in our shame, &c.* They had the meanes of grace, and the Ordinances of God, and shame hath eaten up all, and where are their Temples, and Priviledges now? Shame hath consumed them to nothing. So it is with a poore feeble fainting Soule, he saith, shame hath eaten up all my labours; I have laboured in prayer, in hearing, and in fasting; yet I

have

have no pardon sealed, nor no mercy granted, I am as much troubled as ever; I see as much evill as ever I did; hell is gaping for me, and so soone as life is gone from my body; the devill will have my soule. This is the nature of despaire, to put an impossibility in the thing that it despaires of : and to say, can it be? and will it be? and will it ever be? Nay, it is impossible, for ought I know. Where is the man now, that thought it an easie matter to goe to heaven, he is in another mind, and his heart is of another frame; now he hath found by wofull experience, that there is no hope nor helpe in himselfe nor in the creature.

Secondly, this followes from the former disposi- *The second* tion of spirit; the Soule is restlesse, and remaines *Triall.* unsatisfied in what he hath, and what he doth. The heart cannot be supported, and therefore it growes to be marvellously troubled, and it is not able to stay it selfe. There is nothing that can satisfie the Soule of a man, but it must be some good. No man is satisfied with evill, but rather more troubled with it. It must be some good, either in hand, and in present possession, or else in expectation of some good that he may have, and he saith, it may be, and it will be. But, when he seeth the emptinesse of all his priviledges, and the weakenesse of all his duties; when these faile, his heart and all must needes sinke; because he seeth no other good, but thē; for the while. As it is with the building of a house, if the bottome and foundation be brittle, and rotten, and begin to shake, all the whole building must needs shake: So, the soule that sought for comfort, mercy, and salvation from his outward priviledges and duties; when

I

when all thefe beginne to fhake under him, and to breake in funder, and he feeth no helpe thereby, and that it can receive no eafe therein, hence it is, that the Soule (thus troubled and defpairing) is in fuch an eftate, that if all the Minifters under heaven fhould come to flatter him, and daube him up with untempered mortar, and perfwade him of Gods mercy towards him; Take this man upon his death-bed, when all the Minifters, come to give him comfort upon any termes, and they fay unto him, your courfe hath beene good and commendable, and you have lived thus, and thus; and take much paines in praying, and hearing, and fafting; therefore undoubtedly you cannot but receive mercy from the Lord. See what the poore Soule will reply: It is true (faith he) I have done, and may doe all thefe, but I have not done them in a right manner. I have not had an eye to Chrifts mercy: but have accounted thefe duties, as fatisfactory to Gods juftice, fo that they favour not fo much of dutie, as arrogancie; whileft prefuming upon their worth: I have not depended upon Gods mercy; but even challenged his juftice in the reward of my labours. Thus the Soule argueth with it felfe, I have depended too long upon thefe outward workes, and thought to purchafe heaven by them, but now I finde it neceffary, that I get them dyed, and fanctified in the blood of Chrift. Thus it was with Saint *Paul* when he fayd; *I know nothing by my felfe* · What might fome fay, *Paul*, You are a reverend learned man, and have had a great name in the Church, and who can fay, blacke is your eye. It is true, (faith he) I know nothing by my felfe: but

1 Cor 4 4

what

what then, yet I am not thereby juflified. Nay, it is the difference that he makes betweene himfelfe a Pharifee, and himfelf a poore contrite finner. When he was a Pharifee he counted his priviledges gaine to him; but now *he thought them loff in regard of* Phil. 3. 7. *Chrift.* They are good mercies, where God gives them in regard of themfelves, but in the way of Iuftification, and Salvation, they are as dung and droffe in refpect of any merit in them. This is one difference betweene a dead hypocrite, and a living Chriftian. A dead hypocrite will be content with dead hearing, and dead praying, and with the bare fhell of duties, but, a living Chriftian that feeth his owne evill, and finne; cannot be fild nor contented without a Chrift. That which will maintaine a Camelion, will ftarve a man; for a Camelion will live upon the ayre; but, put a Man into the beft ayre that is, and it will ftarve him, if hee have no other food. So, if thou canft feed upon the ayre of hearing, and the picture, and fhadow of praying; it is a figne thou art a dead man; whereas if thou bee a true man in Chrift Iefus, thou muft have bread, or elfe all the world cannot content thee. Bread for the Lords fake, faith the hunger-ftarved man: therefore let me give thee an Item this way; goe thy way home, and take notice of thine heart, thou that canft licke thy Soule whole, and cure all thy finnes with a few prayers, and teares, and faftings, and in meane time feeft thou not a neceffitie of a Saviour, know that it is a notorious figne of a cunning hypocrite, as there are many in thefe dayes. It is with an hypocrite, as it is with fome men written of in Stories,

I 2

ries, they have such an antidote, and preservative, that they can eate poyson, and it shall never hurt them: So it is with some hypocrites, that have their reservations of some sins, and they retaine some base distempers, and they will tipple in a corner, and lye in some secret sinnes, and yet they trust so much to their antidote, and to their duties, that it will cure all; and it is but praying, and fasting so much the more often. The God of heaven open the eyes, and awaken the consciencies of all such, if there be any such here this day. If it be so that thou canst pray, and keepe a close hollow heart, and thou canst licke thy selfe whole, and then sinne, and a little prayer will serve againe; and then goe, and be unjust, and unclean, and keepe false ballance still, know then, it is certaine thou never hadst a part in Christ, nor ever didst see a need of Christ. And as it was with the Prodigall: if he had beene a Hog, the huskes might have served him; but he was a Man, and therefore must have bread. Therefore thou hypocrite to thy Stye, if these huskes will save thee, and serve thy turne, and if the mill of a prayer will serve, (I doe not discommend these duties : No, cursed be hee that doth it) but if thou content thy selfe with a mill of praying, and yet there is as much power of Christ, and sap of grace in thy heart, as in a chip, then I say thou art a Hog and no Man, whom these huskes will content.

The third Triall.

Thirdly he that seeth himselfe helples and hopelesse in the means, he will constantly labour to goe beyond all the meanes. Because he is in neede and finds no helpe here, he wil seek it else where that his

heart

heart may be refreshed, when the Lord hath awak-
ned the heart, and shewed him the emptinesse of all
means, it makes the soule goe farther than the means:
this is the heavenly skill. It is with the Soule in this
case as it is with a Marriner; though his Land bee
upon the oare, yet he ever lookes homeward to
the haven where he would be. And it is in professing
as it is in trading. You know when a man sets up for
himselfe and would live of his calling, he will buy
and sell, but his eye is ever upon the gaine, thats it
which must keepe the Cart on wheeles, or else hee
may die a begger and shall never be able to keep him
and his, it is not enough to trade, and to buy and sell,
but hee goes beyond all these, and labours to get
something. Iust so it is in professing; it is like thy
trading; thou hearest, and prayest, and professest, but
the gaine is to have Christ made to thee in life and
death gaine; so that, all the gaine a man gets is
Christ. Thou art a professour, and hast beene baptized and hast received the Sacrament, but, what hast
thou gotten by all thy praying, and preaching, and
other services? unlesse thou hast gotten Christ, thou
hast gotten iust nothing at all. It is with thee as it is
with a man that hath a great shop, and much wares,
and quicke returne, and yet he is not able to pay his
debts: so thou performest many faire duties, and
hast many rich priviledges, and yet thou art not a-
ble to satisfie Gods Iustice; nor to recompence the
Church for the wrong done to it, and when thou art
going the way of all flesh, but especially in the day of
judgement, then shall people say of thee, such a man
was buying and selling, and professing all his life,

and yet got nothing; and when a poore Soule is
breathing out his laſt, then comes juſtice, and ſaith,
give me my own, thou haſt ſinned, & therefore thou
muſt die for it; Lord (ſaith he) take ſome prayers,
and readings, and faſtings, in ſtead of payment, and
if theſe will not ſerve, then he is blanke, and juſtice
carries him downe to the place of execution, and he
ſhall not come thence till he have payd the utmoſt
farthing. And then the Soule ſaith, ſome comfort,
ſome mercy and conſolation for me; oh ſaith he, I
have received the Sacrament, & prayed, and faſted,
and profeſſed, canſt thou not feed on theſe? oh no!
(ſaith the Soule) theſe are huskes, bread for me : as
the world thinkes of a man that hath got nothing
by his tradings, ſuch a man that made wonderfull
ſhew in the world to day, ſo many hundreds, and
thouſands worſe than nothing, this is lamentable.
Iuſt ſo it will be with thee, if thou haſt not gotten
Chriſt. If a man have gotten Chriſt in his hearing,
and praying; he will anſwere all eaſily, and when the
Devill comes in, and ſaith; Thou haſt many ſinnes,
who ſhall ſatisfie Gods Iuſtice for them? The ſoule
makes this anſwere; Chriſt hath payd all. Oh, but
thou haſt broken the Law of God (ſaith the devill,)
Oh (ſaith the Soule) Chriſt hath fulfilled all righteouſneſſe for me. You have many corruptions
(ſaith the devill;) but Chriſt hath purged me (ſaith
the Soule.) Oh, but you ſhall be damned (ſaith the
devill to him;) Nay, (ſaith the Soule) there is no
condemnation to them that are in Chriſt, but I am
in Chriſt, and therefore ſhall not be damned. Thus
the Devill ſhall goe away aſhamed, and ſay, That
                                             man

man is out of my reach, I fhall never get him downe
to hell, he hath gotten Chrift.

But here this queftion muft be asked, how may a *Queft.*
man goe beyond himfelfe in all his duties?

Becaufe this is a skill above all skills, therefore *Anfwer.*
for the anfwere hereof take thefe three directions.

Firft, labour to fee an abfolute neceffity of a Chrift *The firft Di-*
in all thefe priviledges that thou haft, and in all the *rection.*
duties and fervices that thou performeft. Firft, in
all thy priviledges; See a need of Chrift to make all
thefe powerfull to thy Soule. Hearing, and reading,
and fafting, will doe thee no good, except thou have
a Chrift to goe with all thefe. As a Ship that hath
faire Sailes, & ftrong Mafts, except there be a winde
it can never goe. So, the Soule is like the Ship; and
the precious ordinances of God are faire Sailes and
good Mafts; and it is good hearing, and good reading, and good fafting; but except the Spirit blow
with thefe, thou canft get no good by them : the
Spirit bloweth where it lifteth, and except the Lord
Iefus Chrift, by the power of his Spirit, goe and
breath upon thy hearing, Preaching, and upon all
the ordinances, they can do thee no good. When the
Lord was to come into his Garden, which was the
Church; The Spices are the graces of Gods Spirit.
The Spices could not grow, becaufe the Spirit
would not blow upon them, and therefore the *Cant. 4. 16.*
Spoufe faith, *Arife oh North, and come (oh South)*
and blow on my Garden, that the Spices thereof may
flow out. As if he had fayd, good Lord, blow this
way, and that way, and give a bleffing to the means,
and then comfort will come indeed. And as there is
neede

need of Chrift to bleſſe all meanes, ſo ſecondly there is need of Chrift to make all thy ſervices acceptable to God the Father. Oh ſend to heaven for Chrift, that he may hide all thy wickedneſſes, and preſent al thy duties to God his Father, in his merits and righteouſnẽſſe. They that brought a Sacrifice in the time of the Law, were to offer it upon the golden Altar, and no Sacrifice was accepted without it: So, if thou wilt have thy hearing, and praying, and faſting acceptable to God, lay them upon the golden Altar, the Lord Ieſus Chrift. And know that thou haſt neede of Chrift to cover all the failings and weakeneſſes in thy duties.

The ſecond Direction.

Secondly, in all the beauty and excellencie of Gods ordinances that thou ſeeſt and prizeſt. See a greater beauty and excellencie in the Lord Ieſus Chrift, than in all theſe. See what comfort is it that thou wouldeſt finde, and what ſweete is it that thou wouldeſt get from hearing, and reading, praying, and profeſſing: goe beyond all this, and ſay, if the beames be ſo ſweete, what is the Sunne it ſelfe, and if the ordinances of God be ſo ſweet and comfortable, what is the Lord Ieſus Chrift then? You come to heare, and it is well that you will come; What would you have in hearing? You would have ſome life to quicken you, and ſome wiſedome in your minds to direct you, and ſome grace into your Soules to purge you; and then me thinkes I heare you ſay, Bleſſed be the Lord, this day I found my heart ſomething more quickned, & my ſoule ſomething inabled to hate ſinne, and to walke with God; bleſſe God for that. But, is a little life in the Word

ſo

so good, and is a little grace in the Sacrament so
sweete, Oh then away, away higher, if these bee so
sweete, what is the Lord Jesus the God of all wisedome, grace, and power. If the Word doe so much
quicken thy Soule, what would the Lord Jesus doe,
if thou couldst get thy heart poissessed of him. Let
all those drops of life and mercy draw up thy heart
to heaven. When the Spouse in the Canticles had
sought after her beloved, see how she describes him,
He is white and ruddie, and so forth; and in the 16. Can. 5.10.16.
verse she saith, *his mouth is most sweete, yea, he is altoge-*
ther lovely. The originall hath it, he is altogether
pleasant, yea, pleasantnesse it selfe. You have some
comfort, and some discomfort with it, you have
some wisedome, and some folly, some power, and
some weakenesse with it; but the Lord Jesus is all
comfort, and no discomfort; he is all power, and no
weakenesse; he is all life, and no deadnesse; therefore
in all the ordinances of God, carry your hearts a
little higher, and looke upon that fulnesse that is in
Christ.

Thirdly, let us labour in the use of all meanes, as The third
to see the beauty of a Christ surpassing all meanes; meanes.
so let us be led by all meanes into a neerer union
with the Lord Christ. As a wife deales with the
letters of her husband that is in a farre Country; she
findes many sweet inklings of his love, and she will
read these letters often, and dayly: she would talke
with her husband a farre off, and see him in the letters, Oh (saith she) thus and thus he thought when
he writ these lines, and then she thinkes he speakes to
her againe; she reades these letters onely, because she

K   would

would be with her husband a little, and have a little parley with him in his pen, though not in his presence: so these ordinances are but the Lords loveletters, and we are the Ambassadors of Christ; and though we are poore sottish ignorant men, yet wee bring mervailous good newes that Christ can save all poore broken hearted sinners in the world.

You doe well to come and heare, but it is all that you may chat and parley a little with Christ. Our Saviour saith, *where the carkasse or the dead body is, there will the Eagles be.* This is the nature of an Eagle, she will not goe to catch flies, (that's the nature of the hedge Sparrow,) but she will prey upon the carkasse. So, this is a good heart that will not prey upon dead duties, but upon the Lord Christ, who is the life of the Soule. If thou art of a right brood, thou wilt not fill and glut thy soule with a few duties like a hedge Sparrow; still, mistake me not; I doe not dispraise these duties, but (I say) they are nothing in the way of justification: if faith in Christs merits be not joyned with them. Therefore if thou hast a dungill heart of thine owne, thou mayest goe and content thy selfe with profession, and with a few cold dead duties; but if thou art an Eagle, and a sound hearted Christian, and one, that God hath beene pleased to doe good unto: thou wilt never be but where the Lord Jesus is, and where his grace and mercy is. As we doe at a Feast; the dish is greater than the meate, yet we reach the dish (not for the dishes sake) but that we may cut some meate: So, the ordinances of God, are as so many dishes, wherein the Lord Jesus Christ is dished out to us. Some-

times

Marginal note: Matth. 24. 28.

times Chrift in his merits, is dished out in the Sacrament to all the senses, and sometimes hee is dished out in the Word; therefore as you take the dish to cut some meate, So, take the Word; that Communicates Chrift to the eare; and prayer Communicates with Chrift, and the Sacrament Communicates Chrift to all the senses; cut the meate, and let not the Lord Chrift goe whole from the Table, and no man looke after him; fill your hungry Soules with Chrift. When a poore travelling man comes to the Ferry; he cries to the other side; Have over, have over; his meaning is, he would goe to the other side by a Boat; he onely desires the use of the Ferryman to convey him over. So, Chrift is in heaven, but we are here on earth (as it were) on the other side of the River: the ordinances of God are but as so many Boats to carry us, and to land us at Heaven where our hopes are; and our hearts should bee. Therefore you would be landed: Have over, have over (saith the Soule.) The Soule desires to bee landed at the Staires of Mercy, and saith, Oh, bring me to speake with my Saviour. *Mary* came to the Sepulchre to seeke for Chrift, and therefore when the Angel sayd to her, *Woman why weepest thou?* she made this answere, *Oh, they have taken away my Lord.* So it is with you, if you be not hypocrites. Is there ever a *Mary* here? is there ever a man or woman that prizeth a Chrift, and seeth need of a Chrift, and that comes weeping and mourning to the holy ordinances of God? whom seekest thou (saith the Word, and Prayer, and the Sacrament? Oh (saith the broken hearted sinner) they have taken away my

Ioh. 20. 13.

K 2   Lord

Lord Chriſt? Oh this ſinnefull heart of mine; oh
theſe curſed corruptions of mine! if it had not beene
for theſe, Chriſt would have comforted my conſcience and pardoned my ſinne; if thou ſeeſt my Chriſt
and my Saviour, reveale him to my Soule, that I
may receive comfort and conſolation by him. This
is the frame of a Chriſtian Soule: when the Ferry-
man hath carried the traveller over, he ſtayes not
there, but goes to the houſe of his friend, and ſaith,
is ſuch a man within, he deſires to ſpeake with him,
and to receive ſome good from him. We heare, and
pray, and reade till we are weary, we doe not cry;
Have over : let me come to enjoy a neerer Com-
munion with my Saviour, that I may dwell with
him, and have a neerer cut to the Lord Chriſt; I
would have way, that I may receive grace and mercy from Chriſt according to my neceſſities. When
a man hath gotten ſo many hundred pounds, he not
onely tels that he hath met with the Ferry-man, but
he ſhewes the money hee hath gotten. So you
come to Church, and goe from Church, and you
have your hearing, for your hearing; and your profeſſing for your profeſſing, and the like; but you
ſhould labour to ſay, I have gotten the pardon of
all my ſinnes, and the aſſurance of Gods love to my
Soule; I have beene with my Saviour, and thus graciouſly, and mercifully hee hath dealt with mee.
All that I have ſayd, is but a ſpeech of little time,
but it is a taske for all a mans life. Oh thinke of it,
and ſay, what have I gotten by all that I have done?
and ſay, what would I get when I go to prayer? I would
have a Chriſt and mercy from him. This is not in
                                                      our

our minds. I tell thee what thou muſt aime at, and
labour for, heare, and pray for a Saviour. See a neede
of Chriſt in all, and ſee greater beautie in Chriſt
then in all, and be led neerer to Chriſt by all, or
elſe you get nothing by all that you doe. If there
were no gold in the Weſt-Indies the King of *Spaine*
would not care for his Shippes, nor for that place.
Schoole-boyes care not for the Carrier, but for letters from a Father. So, now raiſe up your hearts
higher towards heaven : All holy duties are but as
ſhips, and Carriers; but the golden Mines of Mercy
are all in the Lord Jeſus Chriſt. It was a ſweet ſpeech
of a man (whether he was good or bad I know not)
that a man ſhould loſe the creatures in God. So, I
would have you doe, loſe your ſelves and all ordinances, and creatures, and all that you have, and do,
in the Lord Chriſt, How is that? Let all be ſwallowed up, and let nothing be ſeene but a Chriſt, and
let thy heart be ſet upon nothing but a Chriſt. As
it is with the Moone and Starres, when the Sunne
comes, they looſe all their light, though they are
there in the heavens ſtill; and as it is with Rivers,
they all goe into the ſea, and are all ſwallowed up
of the Sea : and yet there is nothing ſeene but the
Sea. So, all the ordinances, and creatures, are
as ſo many Rivers from that Ocean of mercy and
goodneſſe in Chriſt, and they all returne thither;
therefore onely ſee a Fountaine of grace, goodneſſe,
wiſedome, and power in Chriſt : When a man is
upon the Sea, he can ſee no freſh water, it is all ſwallowed up : So let it be with thy Soule, when thou
wouldeſt finde mercy and grace. The ordinances of

God

God are good in themselves, yet lose them all in
Chrift. That wisedome in Chrift is able to direct,
and that grace and mercy in Chrift is able to save,
when all other helpes faile, and that power of Chrift
muft-support the Soule in time of trouble. There
is some comfort and sweete, and some refreshing in
the Word, and in the Sacrament,and in the company of Gods people; but loose all these in the Lord
Chrift. And see that mercy, and compassion,and that
boundlesse goodnesse that is in the Lord Jesus; and
that mercy that will pardon all sinnes, and forgive
all forts of sinners, if they be humbled before him.
There is no pardon in grace,nor in meanes,in Word,
nor in Sacraments, there is none but in Chrift, see
none but that; and when thou art there, hold thy
heart to it; drench and drowne thy Soule there, and
fling thy Soule into the Sea of that plenteous Redemption in Chrift; and though thy prayers and
all faile, yet that mercy in Chrift will never faile.
Away with these Rivers, these are all fresh-water.
comforts that will faile; but that Sea of mercy in
Chrift will hold for ever. See a Sea of misery and
confusion in thy soule, and a Sea of mercy in Chrift
and say,none but that Lord; Heere sit, and here fall,
and for ever establish thy soule, that it may goe well
with thee for ever. Thus you ought to goe beyond
all meanes; and he that doth thus doth truely despaire of all saving succour in them. Therefore goe
home, and say thus, the Lord hath given mee some
comfort, and some grace, and a heart enlarged to
walke with God, and to performe duty, to him, but
I truft not in this comfort, nor in my enlargement,all
                                                    my

my comfort is in Chrift, that Sea of mercy is ftill
full, and I reft there; goe from all thefe to that, and
reft there,' and let that content thee for ever,

Thus you fee how farre the Prodigall hath gone.
What doth he now? he comes to himfelfe and faith,
I will arife and goe to my Father, and fay to him, Father,
I have finned againft heaven and before thee, and am no
more worthy to be called thy Sonne, make me as one of
thy hyred Servants. Now his ftout ftomacke is come
downe, and he comes home by weeping croffe, and
he that had formerly flighted the kindneffe of a father, and fayd, He would not alwayes bee holden
within his fathers houfe, he would have his portion,
and he hath it, and is gone, and at laft when his heart
and all failes him, he comes to himfelf and fayd, here
I may ftarve and dye too, the hogs fare better than I
doe, therefore home I will goe to my father, &c.

This is the third paffage that I told you of in the
defcription of this worke of humiliation.

In thefe words there are thefe two things cleare.

Firft, he fubmits himfelfe to his father.

Secondly, he is content to be at his fathers difpofing; he doth not feeke to be his owne carver, and
fay, if I may be my fathers fteward, and have fome
eminent place in the houfe, then I will goe home, no,
but he faith, father, I am not worthy to be a Sonne,
make me as a hired fervant, if I can but get into my
fathers houfe againe; I will dye rather than goe away
any more: he is content to be any thing, fo his father
will but receive him into his family, though it were
but to be a drudge in the kitchen, heres a heart worth
gold; oh! (faith he) let all the weight lye upon me, I
care

care not what I be, only let me be a servant. So then from the former of these two, the Doctrine is this.

The distressed sinner that despaires of all supply and succour in himselfe, is driven to submit himselfe to the Lord God for succour and releefe.

It is no thankes to the Prodigall that he comes home now, neither is it any thankes to a poore sinner that he returnes after all his wandring away from God, yet better late than never. For the opening of this point I will shew two things.

First, What is the behaviour of the heart in this worke of submission, and the manner of it.

Secondly, the reasons why the Lord drives the heart to this stand, and makes it fall downe at the footstoole of mercy.

The first, how the Soule behaves it selfe in this subjection. The sinner having a sight of his owne sin and being troubled and overwhelmed with the unsupportable sorrow that attends thereupon, and yet he is not able to get power over his sinne, nor assurance of pardon from the Lord; for you must conceive the sinner to be in the worke of preparation, and yet he conceives God to be an enemie against him, though he is in a good way to mercy, yet God comes as an angry God against him, and he takes what course he can, and seekes far and wide, and improves all meanes and takes up all duties, that (if it were possible) he might heale his wounded Soule, and get ground against his corruptions, but the truth is, he findes no succour, and receives no comfort in what he hath, nor in what he doth, and therefore being in this despairing condition; he seeth he cannot
avoyd

avoyd Gods anger, neither can he beare it, therefore he is forced(though loath)to make tryall of the
kindnesse of a Father, and of the Lord, though for
the present he apprehends God to be just, and to be
incensed against him, and though he hath no experience of Gods favour for the while, and no certaintie
how he shall speed if he come to God; yet because
he sees that he cannot be worse than he is, but hee
may be better if God please,and this he knowes,that
none but God can helpe him:therefore he fals at the
foot-stoole of mercy, and lies grovelling at the gate
of grace, and submits himselfe to God that he may
do what he wil with him. When *Ionah* had denoun-
ced that heavie judgement, and (as it were) throwne
wild-fire about the streetes, saying, *within forty dayes
Nineveh shall be destroyed;* See what they resolve upon, they fasted, and prayed, and put on sack-cloth
and ashes; the Lord in mercy grant that we may take
the like courses, *who can tell* (sayd they) *but God* Ionah.3.9.
*may turne and repent him of his fierce wrath that wee pe-
rish not.* As if they had sayd,we know not what God
will doe, but this we know that we cannot oppose
Gods judgements, nor prevent them, nor succour
our selves : yet who can tell but the Lord may bee
gracious and bountifull,and yet continue peace and
goodnesse to us in this kind; thus it is with a sinner
despairing of all succour in himselfe, when he seeth
hell fire flashing in his face, and that he cannot succour himselfe,then he saith, this I know, that all the
meanes in the world cannot save me, yet who can
tell but the Lord may have mercy upon mee, and
cure this distressed conscience, and heale all these
L   wounds

wounds that finne hath made in my Soule: when *Paul* went breathing out threatnings againſt the Church of God, and he came furniſhed with letters from the high Prieſts, with all his trickes and implements to perſecute the Saints; the Lord met him and there was a ſingle combat fought between them the glory of the Lord amazed him, and threw him flat on the ground, and when *Paul* ſaw the Lord Jeſus had the advantage againſt him, hee yeelded himſeife and ſayd, *Lord, what wilt thou have me to doe?* This is the lively picture of the Soule in this caſe; this ſubjection diſcovers it ſelfe in foure particulars.

Act. 9 6.

Firſt, take the ſoule deſpairing of mercy and ſuccour in himſelfe, hee ſeeth and confeſſeth that the Lord may, and (for ought he knowes) will proceed in juſtice againſt him, and execute upon him thoſe plagues that God hath threatned, and his ſin deſerved; and he ſeeth that Juſtice is not yet ſatisfied, and all thoſe reckonings betweene God and him are not made up, and therefore he cannot apprehend but that God may, and will take vengeance of him; he ſeeth that when he hath done all that he can, he is unprofitable, and Juſtice remaines unſatisfied, and ſaith, thou haſt ſinned, and I am wronged, and therefore thou ſhalt die. See what the Text ſaith, *can a man be profitable to the Lord?* as he that is wiſe may be profitable to himſelfe, is it any pleaſure to the Almightie that thou art righteous, or is it any gaine to him that thou makeſt thy way perfect. So the Soule ſaith; Is all that I can doe any thing to the Lord, is the Lords Juſtice any gainer by it? Nay, Juſtice is yet unſatisfied, becauſe there is ſinne in all that I doe,

Iob 22 2, 3.

and

and therefore Juſtice may proceede againſt me:there-
fore the ſoule reſolves, that the Lord may and will:
Nay, why ſhould he not come in vengeance, and
Judgement againſt him?

Secondly, he conceives that what God will doe, **2.**
he can doe, and he cannot avoyd it. The anger of
the Lord cannot be reſiſted; If the Lord will come
and require the glory of his Juſtice againſt him,
there is no way to avoyd it, nor to beare it, and this
cruſheth the heart, and makes the ſoule to be beyond
all ſhifts, and evaſions, and all thoſe trickes, whereby
it may ſeeme to avoyd the dint of the Lords blow.
As *Iob* ſaith, *He is one mind, and who can turne him,* Iob 23. 13,14,
and what his ſoule deſireth, that doth he. It is admirable 15,16.
to conſider it: for this is it that makes the heart melt
and come under; When the Soule ſaith, If God
come who can turne him, he will have his honour
from this wretched proud heart of mine, he will
have his glory from me, either here in my humiliation, or elſe hereafter in my damnation. And in the
next verſe, *Iob* ſaith, *Many ſuch things are with him:*
As if he had ſayd, he hath many wayes to cruſh a
carnall confident heart, and to make it lye low, hee
wants not meanes to pull downe even the moſt rebellious ſinner under heaven. And now marke what
followes, He can cruſh them all; What became of
Nimrod, Cain, Pharaoh, and *Nebuchadnezzar;* They
are all brought downe; therefore (ſaith he) I am
troubled at his preſence, when I conſider it; I am
afraid, for God maketh my heart ſoft, and the Almighty troubleth me.

Thirdly, as the ſinner apprehends, that God may **3.**
doe

doe what he will and he cannot refift him: So the
foule flings away all fhifts and tricks that he had, and
he refignes up the power of all his priviledges that
he hath to defend himfelfe withall; he cafts away his
weapons, and falls downe before the Lord, and refignes himfelfe into the Soveraigne power and command of God. This was in the Spirit of the Prophet *David*; When the Lord had caft him out of
his Kingdome, he fayd to *Zadock*, *carry backe the
Arke of God into the Citie, if I fhall finde favour in the
eyes of the Lord, he will bring me backe againe, and
fhew me both it, and his habitation. But if he thus fay
to me, I have no delight in thee, Behold, here I am, let
him doe with me as feemeth good in his eyes.* Or as it
was with thofe people, 2 *Kings* 10. 2, 3, 4. Where
when *Iehu* fent this meffage to the people of *Ifrael*
faying, *Now affoone as this letter commeth to you, feeing your Mafters fonnes are with you, and there are
with you chariots, and armour, und a fenced Citie, looke
out even the beft and fitteft of your Mafters fonnes, and
fet him on his Fathers throne, and fight for your fathers
houfe.* But the Text faith, *they were all exceedingly a-
fraid, and therefore they fent word to* Jehu; *and fayd,
two Kings could not ftand out againft thee, and then how
can we ftand? We are thy fervants, and will doe all that
thou fhalt bid us, we will make no King, doe thou that
which is good in thine eyes.* This is the frame of a poore
Soule: When a poore finner will ftand upon his own
priviledges, the Lord faith, be re my Juftice, and
defend thy felfe by all that thou haft, if thou canft;
and the Soule faith, I am thy fervant (Lord) doe
what is good in thine eyes, I cannot fuccour my felf:
there-

2 Sam. 15.
25, 26.

2 King 10. 2.
3, 4.

therefore the heart gives up it selfe to bee at the command of God.

Fourthly, The Soule thus yeelding up the weapons, and comming in, as to an enemie, and as conquered; then in the last place the Soule freely acknowledgeth, it is in Gods power to doe with him, and to dispose of him as he will; and therefore he lyes and lickes the dust, and cryes mercy, mercy, Lord. He doth not thinke to purchase mercy at the Lords hands, but onely saith; it is onely in Gods good pleasure to doe with him as he will, but hee lookes at his favour, and cryes, mercy (Lord) to this poore distressed soule of mine. And when the Lord heares a sinner come from wandring up and downe in his priviledges, the Lord replyes to the Soule in this manner and saith. Doest thou neede mercy? I had thought thy hearing and praying, and fasting, would have carried thee to heaven without all hazard, therefore gird up thy loynes, and make thy ferventest prayers, and let them meete my Justice, & see if they can beare my wrath and purchase mercy; Nay (saith the sinner) I know it by lamentable experience, I have prooved, that all my prayers and performances, will never procure peace to my soule, nor give any satisfaction to thy Justice, I onely pray for mercy, and I desire onely to heare some newes of mercy, to releeve this miserable and wretched soule of mine; it is onely mercy that must helpe me; Oh mercy, if it may be possible: the issue is thus much; The sinner seeth that all he hath, and can doe, can never succour him, and therefore he throwes away his carnall confidence, and hee submits him-

4.

L 3   selfe·

selfe to the Lord; and now he seeth that the Lord
may justly come against him, and that his Justice is
not satisfied, and that he cannot beare Gods wrath,
nor avoyd it, and he casts away all his shifts, and lies
downe at the gate of mercy. As it is with a debtor
that stands bound for some faire greater summes,
than ever he is able to pay, to satisfie of himselfe
he cannot, and his friends will not : and he knowes
that the bonds are still in force, and his creditor will
sue him; avoyd the suite he cannot, and to beare it,
he is not able; and therefore he comes in freely, and
offers himselfe, and his person, and gives up himselfe into his creditors hands; onely he beseecheth
him to remit that which he can never pay. Just so it
is with the Soule of a poore sinner. The soule *is*
the Debtor : and Divine Justice is the Creditor.
When the poore sinner hath used all meanes to save
and succour himselfe, and to make payment, and hee
hath (as it were) made a gathering of prayers all the
Countrey over, and yet he seeth, that there is a con-
troversie betweene God and him; and yet his sinne
is not pardoned : and God is Just and will have his
honour, and he is not able to avoyd the suite nor to
beare it, and the Son'e saith, as *David* did; *whither*
Psal. 139 7, 8. *shall I goe from thy Spirit? and whither shall I flye from*
thy presence ? If I ascend up into heaven, thou art there,
&c. So the Soule saith, God will have his payment
from this heart blood of mine; if I go into the East,
the Lord will follow mee; and bid his Serjeant
Conscience to arrest me and I shall lye and rot in
the Prison of hell for ever. Now the Soule offers
himselfe before the Lord, and saith, *Father, I have*
sinned

sinned against heaven, and before thee: Oh shew mercy (if it be possible) to this poore distressed Soule of mine: thus the prodigall did, Another similitude is this. Me thinkes the picture of those foure famished Lepers, may fitly resemble this poore sinner. When the famine was great in Samaria. *There were foure leprous men sate in the gate of the Citie, and they sayd, Why sit we here untill we dye? If wee enter into the Citie, the famine is there, and if we sit here we dye also, Now let us therefore fall into the hands of our enemies, if they save us alive we shall live, and if they kill us we shall but dye.* They had but one meanes to succour themselves withall, and that was to goe into the Campe of their enemies, come (sayd they) we will put it to the venture, and so they did, and were releeved: This is the lively picture of a poore sinner in this despairing condition. When the Soule of a poore Leprous sinner is famished for want of comfort, and he seeth the wrath of God pursuing of him, and the Lord besets him on every side : at last he resolves thus with himselfe, I say, when he hath used all meanes, and findes succour in none; he resolves thus with himselfe and saith, if I goe and rest upon my priviledges, there is nothing but emptinesse and weakenesse, if I trust in them; and if I rest in my naturall condition, I perish there also. Let me therefore fall into the hands of the Lord of Hosts, who (I confesse) hath beene provoked by me, and for ought I see is mine enemie, I am now a damned man, and if the Lord cast me out of his presence, I can but be damned that way, and then he comes to the Lord, and falls downe before the footstoole of a

2 King 7 3. 8, 9, &c.

consu-

confuming God, and faith as *Iob* did, *What fhall I
fay unto thee, O thou preferver of men?* I have no reafon to plead for my felf withall, and I have no power to fuccour my felfe, my accufations are my beft
excufe, all the priviledges in the world cannot jufti-
fie me, and all my duties cannot fave me, if there be
any mercy left, Oh fuccour a poore diftreffed finner
in the very gall of bitterneffe. This is the behaviour
of the Soule in this worke of fubjection.

The reafon why the Lord deales thus with the
Soule, and why he pluckes a finner upon his knees,
there is great reafon why he fhould doe it. The reafon is two-fold. Firft, That the Lord may herein ex-
preffe and glorifie the greatneffe of his power. And
fecondly, to fhew forth the glory of his mercy.

1. Reafon.

Firft, the glory of his power is marvelloufly magnified, in that the Lord fhewes that hee is able to
pull downe the proudeft heart, and to lay low the
hautieft fpirits under heaven, and thofe that have
out-braved the God of heaven, and beene oppofite
to him, and defpifed the glory of his Name. For
herein is the glory of his Name greatly exalted, that
he makes a poore wretch to come, and creepe, and
crawle before him, and beg for mercy at his hands,
and to be at his difpofe.

It is a fine paffage. You know how *Pharaoh* would
out-face the Lord, faying, *Who is the Lord that I fhould
obey him?* And as the Mafter fometime faith to his
Exod. 9. 27.
fervant, You fhall, And you fhall doe this, faith the
husband to his wife. This is the fturdy fierceneffe of
a company of wretches. Well, the Lord let him a-
lone for the while, but in the 27. verfe, when the
                                                  Lord

Lord had freed and delivered his servants, and had plagued the Egyptians with the haile, then *Pharaoh* fayd, *Now I know that the Lord is greater than all Gods, and that he is righteous, but I and my people are wicked.* Where is *Pharaoh* and *Nimrod*, and all the reft of thofe mightie ones of the world ? they are all gone downe to hell, and God hath deftroyed them, for, in the thing wherein they dealt proudly hee was above them. Herein is the glory of Gods power. So it is here. As we ufe to fay, Doe you know fuch a man ? Yes. What was he ? A profeft drunkard, and a defperate defpifer of God and his grace, and one that did hate the very face of an honeft man. Oh, the Lord hath brought him upon his knees. Oh, admirable (faith he) what is he humbled, and is his heart broken ? Oh yes, the Lord hath dejected him in that wherein he was proud. As it is amongft men: If two men be in controverfie, and the one enters into fuit with the other, and before a man will fubmit and yeeld himfelfe, he will dye, and rather fpend all that he hath then to want his will, and he will make that tongue deny what it hath fpoken. He thinks this his excellencie : So it is with our God. Herein is the power of the Almighty magnified, that he hath brought down thofe great *Leviathans*; and all thofe *Nimrods* and great Kings, which fayd, Who is the Lord ? he hath made fuch as thefe are, to come in, and to fubmit unto him.

Secondly, by this meanes the Lord doth mar. velloufly promote the praife of his mercy. Firft, partly for the greatneffe of it. And fecondly, partly for the freedome of it, Firft, in that the Lord helpes

The fecond Meanes.

M   a

a poore finner at a dead lift, and when all prayers,
and hearings prevailed not, and when all priviledges
were not able to purchafe mercy and favour, then
the Lord fhewes mercy. Doth not this argue the
excellencie of that Balme? that will cure when all
other meanes cannot doe the deede, that the Lord
fhould then (I fay) looke upon a poore finner, and
refrefh him with one drop of mercy: Oh, this is un-
fpeakable mercy ! As the Prophet *David* faith, *All
my bones can fay, Lord who is like unto thee ?* as if hee
had fayd, This eye that hath wept for my finnes, this
tongue that hath confeft my finnes, and this heart
that hath grieved for finne, all thefe have beene refrefhed by thee. This prayer is not like to thee, this
fafting and thefe priviledges are not like to thee, for
thefe could not fuccour me; but thou art the Lord
that didft deliver and fuccour thy poore fervant.
And fecondly, herein is alfo admirable freeneffe of
mercy; that when the Lords mercy was but lightly
looked after, that then the Lord fhould give mercy,
and that to an enemie. For, the Soule can fay, if any
thing in the world would have faved me, I fhould
not have gone to the Lord for mercy; and yet when
all would not doe, and when I did not thinke of any
fuch matter, then the Lord faved me. This is free
mercy. The hope of *Ifrael* is not like others, and the
God of *Iacob* is not like other Gods. You diftreffed
Soules, did not you know the time when God terrified you, and then offered mercy and you would
none, but you would fcramble for mercy, and fhift
for your owne comfort, and yet the Lord brought
downe thofe proud hearts of yours, and when you
were

were at a dead lift, and could finde comfort no where
elſe, then did the Lord ſhew mercy to your Soules.
Was not this free mercy? wonder at it, and give
God glory for it, even for ever.

This being ſo, that the ſoule that is throughly *Vſe.* 1.
humbled, yeelds to ſubmit it ſelfe to the Lord: Then,
this is like a Bill of inditement againſt all the ſtout
ones of the world. This ſhewes how unworthy they
are of any mercy; Nay, how unfit they are for mercy. They are ſo farre from partaking of Gods mercy, that they will not be humbled, and therefore
they cannot be exalted: Nay, they have a baſe e-
ſteeme of it, and ſo they hate their everlaſting ſalvation. For, looke how farre they are from ſubmiſſion,
ſo farre they are from the comfort and happineſſe
of the Lord. He that will enter in at the ſtraite gate
of ſubjection, is ſo farre from ever going in the way
to life; that he never ſet one foote (yet) in this way.
Let me ſpeake, as once the Prophet did; *Heare and
tremble all you ſtout ones of the earth, you that account
it a matter of credit to caſt off the Commandements of
God, and that you can lift up your ſelves againſt the Almightie.* Good Lord, is it poſſible? you know what
I ſay; there is many a one here, and if they be not
here, (as commonly they are not) let them heare of
it. How is it that men ſlight all corrections, and
ſnap all Gods Cōmandements in ſunder, as *Samſon*
did the cords; and they ſay, their tongues are their
owne, and their luſts are the commands that carry
them: Nay, is it come to this paſſe now adayes
(for the Lords ſake thinke of it) that men account
it a matter of baſeneſſe of ſpirit to be ſuch childiſh

M 2   babes,

babes, and to be ſo womanniſh, as to ſtoope a every
command. Oh, you muſt not be drunke, (ſaith one)
it is a hot argument, and are you ſuch a child as to
yeeld to it. No, let us follow our owne wayes; is
it not thus? I appeale to your owne Soules: there
are too many guilty in this place: Doe you thinke
to out-brave the Almighty in this manner? Doe
you provoke the Lord to wrath, and doe you not
provoke your ſoules to your owne confuſion?
Doeſt thou thinke to goe to heaven thus bolt upright, the Lord cannot indure thee here, and will
He ſuffer thee to dwell with himſelfe for ever in
heaven? What, thou to heaven upon theſe termes?
Nay, thou muſt not thinke to out-brave the Lord in
this manner, and to go to heaven too? How did the
Lord deale with *Lucifer*, and all thoſe glorious ſpirits? He ſent them all downe to hell for their pride.
Let all ſuch ſpirits heare, and know their miſerie. I
doe not trouble my ſelfe with any matter of indignation, it is no trouble to me, but onely becauſe of
your ſinnes, for you are the greateſt objeƈts of pitty
under heaven. You that know ſuch, and have ſuch
husbands: oh mourne for them exceedingly. The
Lord doth deteſt their perſons. As the Wiſe man
ſaith; *The froward in heart are an abhomination to the
Lord.* The Lord doth abhorre that heart of thine:
And, ſhall God abhominate that proud heart of
thine, and yet bleſſe it, and ſave it, and will he dwell
with ſuch a heart in heaven? No, he hath ſome body
elſe to give heaven to. Secondly, thy eſtate is deſperate here, and marvellous unrecoverable. As the
ſame Wiſeman ſaith, *He that being often reprooved,*
harde-

Prov. 11.20.

*hardeneth his necke, and will not ftoope to any counfels,
nor reproofes,* but faith : Who meddles with you, and
I know what I have to doe, and let every Tub ftand
upon his owne bottome. How many of you here
have beene reprooved for your fwearing, but you
leave it not? How many of you have beene reprooved for your prophaning of the Lords Day? doe
you withdraw your felves from it? Oh no fuch matter! Goe your wayes then and mourne over thofe
hard hearts of yours; and in private fay thus. This
is my fentence right. The Lord be mercifull to my
Father (faith the childe) and the Lord bee mercifull
to my proud husband, (faith the wife) and to my
wife, (faith the husband,) are not we they that have
beene often reprooved? have not wee had fuch ex-
hortations as have made the Church to fhake; the
devils would have gotten more good if they had
had them, and yet we have caft off all, and we would
not come in; we doe not yet pray in our Families,
but we throw away all; the Lord hath fayd it, hee
that being often reprooved hardneth his necke, and
will not come in, fhall perifh : he is gone then, and
therefore thou mayft fay, Oh my husband is but a
dead man, and my child is a dead child, hee fhall
perifh : but there is no remedie, (may fome fay)
No, the Text faith fo, he fhall fuddenly be deftroyed, and that without remedie. The truth is, I neede
fay no more, but that you know your owne hearts;
bewaile thofe hard hearts of yours, that (as the water
by continuall dropping, at laft melts the flint) fo if
it be poffible, thofe proud hearts of yours may bee
brought downe. If a drunkard, or an adulterer will

fubmit

submit to the Word, there is remedy for them; but there is no remedie for him, that will not yeeld to the Spirit of God. The Lord be mercifull to the Soules of them. Will you see your sturdie hearted husbands and children perish? the Lord in mercy set this home to your hearts at last, and prevaile with them. Will you perish, and that suddenly? Oh let us pitty them! will you not yeeld now, but will you stand it out to the last man?

The Lord comes out in battell array against a proud person, and singles him out from all the rest, and when the Vialls of his wrath are powred out upon all wicked ones, (me thinkes) the Lord saith, Let that drunkard and that swearer alone a while, but let me destroy that proud heart for ever. You shall submit in spight of your teeth, when the great God of heaven and earth shall come to execute vengeance, and doe not thinke to scarre God with your mocks, you that will sweare a man out of your company. Consider that place in *Iob*, and see how the Lord comes with all his full might against a proud man. It is good to read this place often, that God may pull downe our proud hearts. *For he stretcheth* *out his hands against the Almighty* (saith the text) *and strengthneth himselfe against God,* and he saith, *I will doe it though my life lye at the stake for it,* he strengthens himselfe and will doe it. Surely God is afraid of him, he comes so well mann'd; the Lord must deale some way with him to overthrow him. Marke what the text saith; *The Lord runnes upon him even on his necke, upon the thicke bosses of his bucklers, because he covereth his face with his fatnesse, and maketh collops*
of

Iob 15. 25,
26, 27.

of fat upon his flankes; the Lord comes upon him not at the advantage, but in the height of his pride, and in the rage of his malice the Lord will come upon him, and ruinate him for ever: Those that now stand it out, and cast off all, carelesly throwing away the Commandements of God; I would have them at the day of their death to out-stand the curse of God. The Lord God commands to sanctifie his Sabbaths, and to love his truth and his children, yet, you will not, but you will strive against all; I would have you to out-stand the curse of God in the day of Judgement, and when the Lord Jesus shall say, *Depart from me, ye cursed, into everlasting fire*, stand it out now, and say, I will not goe to hell (Lord) I will not be damned, No, no; you broke the cords here, but the Lord will bind you in chaines of darkenesse for ever, remove those chaines if you can. No, *the* Esay. 2. 17. *haughtiest of men shall be brought low, and the loftinesse of men shall be abased, and the Lord shall onely be exalted in that day.*

The second Use is for instruction, to shew unto us *Vse.* 2. that an humble Soule is marvellous teachable and tractable, and is willing to yeeld unto, and to bee guided by any truth; it submits, and there is no quarrelling against the Commandements of God, one word of Gods mouth is enough. If the Lord reprooves, it takes the same home to it selfe, if the Lord promiseth, it beleeves; and if the Lord threatens, it trembles. It is easie to be convinced of whatsoever it is informed, if it have no good reason to gaine-say it. It is not of that wayward and pettish disposition, that it will not be satisfied though all
his

his reasons be answered, and all objections taken away. It is not led by his owne humours, as many a man is, though his conceits be against reason, and opposite against God and his grace. Nay, it is content to yeeld to the authoritie of the truth, and to take the impression of every truth; it heares, and yeelds, and obeyes, and frames it selfe answerably. As *Iob* saith, *That which I know not teach thou me, and if I have done any iniquitie, I will doe so no more.* The humble Soule is content to confesse his ignorance, and to submit to any truth, that may informe him, and it is content to receive that mercy and grace that is offered, by what meanes soever God seeth best to Communicate it. Nay, the heart that is truely submissive, is as willing to take comfort when it is offered upon good grounds, as it is to performe dutie enjoyned. By a foolish pettishnesse, the devill withdrawes the hearts of Gods owne people from much comfort, that God hath dished out of purpose for their benefit. For howsoever the Soule of a poore sinner be truely touched, yet for want of this lowlinesse, and this teachablenesse, and submission it refuseth, that sap and sweete, that it should take and receive from the Lord. Take a poore sinner, that hath many sinnes burthening of him, and hee is crushed with them, and that in truth he desires comfort, but receives none: Let the Minister of God come, and answere all his arguments, and satisfie all his quarrels that he can make, and set him on a cleare boord, and tell him that the worke of grace is cleare, and mercy is appointed for him: Now marke how he flyes off through that sullennesse, and untoward

peevish-

Iob 34.32.

peeviſhneſſe and pride of Spirit, he caſts away the
mercy, and yeelds not to the comfort offered, though
he is content to yeeld to the duties enjoyned, and ſo
he deprives himſelfe of that mercy, and comfort
that is offered; and thus when all is done time after
time, the Soule ſaith, I ſee it not, and I perceive it
not: and all the world ſhall not perſwade me of it.
Why? what, are you wiſer than all the world?
what a pride of heart is this? Oh ſaith he, another
man may be cozened and deceived, but I know my
owne heart better then any Miniſter doth. But you
tell the Miniſter what your condition is, and ſo,
what you know hee knowes, and hee hath more
judgement, to enforme you, then you have of your
ſelfe. Then ſaith the Miniſter, all your cavils and
objections are anſwered, and remooved; and all
that worke of grace that God hath wrought, you
have made it knowne and revealed, and all this is
made good by the Word of God; now, if all theſe
quarrels be anſwered, and if all the reaſons and evidences of the worke of grace be made cleare, that
you cannot deny them; then, why may not you
take comfort? Downe with that proud heart of
yours that will not beleeve, whatſoever the Miniſter ſaith. Oh the height of pride, and haughtineſſe
of heart in this caſe! I ſpeake to you to whom comfort and mercy is impropriated; downe with thoſe
proud ſpirits I ſay. It is not becauſe you cannot, but
becauſe you will not. It is ſayd in *Eſay*, God prepares Eſa. 61. 3.
the garment of gladneſſe for the ſpirit of heavineſſe.
When the Lord ſeeth the ſoule prepared and humbled, he takes meaſure of it, and diſheth out a com-

N

fort

fort anfwerable, hee prepares a confolation as fit as
may be, and yet the Soule will not put it on, nor bee
warmed and refrefhed with it; as it is with fome
way-ward and untoward child, who when his father
hath prepared a fuite of cloathes fitting for him; becaufe he hath not fuch and fuch a lace, he will not
put it on, but throwes it away. Oh, it is marvellous pride of fpirit ! a rod, a rod. Even fo, when the
Lord prepares the garment of gladneffe, you will
not put it on, nor receive the comfort that is offered,
and fo fwelt your owne hearts.

Now I come to this laft paffage in this worke of
Humiliation, and this is the dead lift of all. The
Prodigall doth not ftand it out with his Father and
fay, I am now come againe, if I may have halfe the
rule in the Family, I am content to live with you.
No, though hee would not ftay there before, yet
now he cannot be kept out, he is content to bee any
thing. Oh (faith he) I confeffe I doe deferve the
worft, but if any man will once helpe mee in, and
but throw mee over the threfhold, if I may but
Scoure the Kettles, or doe any drudgery, I will
never out againe. Oh that I could get in once! As if
he had fayd, you that thinke nothing fufficient, if
you had tafted the bitterneffe of affliction as I have
done, you would be glad of any thing in a fathers
houfe : Come all you drunkards, and adulterours,
you will needes away from God, and his grace? I
tell you, if you were bitten and troubled as I have
beene, then you would fay, it is good being in a fathers houfe, and it is good yeelding to the Lord upon any termes : as it is with this Prodigall : So it
                                                    is.

is with every foule that is truely humbled with the
fenfe of his owne vilenesse. When the Soule feeth
that no duties will quiet his confcience, nor get the
pardon of his finne, he comes home and is content,
not onely to take up the profeffion of the Gofpell
upon fome agreements with the Lord, and to fay, if
I may have honours, and preferments, and eafe, and
liberty, and the like, then I am content to follow it.
Nay, the Soule faith, let me be a miferable flave and
imprifoned, let me be a fervant, and be brought to
the heavieft hazzards, I care not what I be, if the Lord
will but receive me to mercy. Lord (faith he) fhew
me mercy, and I am content to be, and to fuffer any
thing. So from hence the Doctrine is this.

The Soule that is truly humbled, is content to be difpofed
of by the Almighty, as it pleafeth him.

4.
Doctrine.

The maine pitch of this point lyes in the word,
content. This phrafe is a higher pitch than the former of fubmiffion: and this is plaine by this example. Take a debtor, who hath ufed all meanes to a-
voyd the creditor: in the end he feeth that hee cannot avoyd the fuit, and to beare it hee is not able.
Therefore the onely way is to come in, and yeeld
himfelfe into his creditors hands; where there is
nothing, the King muft loofe his right; fo the debtor yeelds himfelfe: but fuppofe the creditor fhould
ufe him hardly, exact the uttermoft, and throw him
into prifon; Now to be content to under-goe the
hardeft dealing, it is a hard matter: this is a further
degree than the offering himfelfe. So, when the
Soule hath offered himfelfe, and he feeth that Gods
writs are out againft him, and his Confcience (the

Lords Serjeant) is comming to ferve a *Subpœna* on
him, and it is not able to avoyd it, nor to beare it
when he comes, therefore he fubmits himfelfe and
faith, Lord, whither fhall I goe, thy anger is heavie
and unavoydable; Nay, whatfoever God requires,
the Soule layes his hand upon his mouth, and goes
away contented and well fatisfied, and it hath nothing to fay againft the Lord. This is the nature of
the Doctrine in hand, and for the better opening of
it, let me difcover three things.

1.   Firft What is the behaviour of the Soule, in this
worke, of contentedneffe. Brethren, thefe are paffages of great weight, that I would have every man to
take notice of.

2.   Secondly, What is the behaviour of the Lord,
or, what is the difpofition wherewith the Soule
muft be contented.

3.   Thirdly, The reafon why the Lord will have the
heart at fuch an under, and to be at his command ?
For, howfoever the Lords worke is fecret in other
ordinary things, yet all the Soules that ever came
to Chrift, and that ever fhall come to Chrift, muft
have this worke upon them; and it is impoffible that
faith fhould be in the Soule; except this worke bee
there firft, to make way for faith.

How fhall a man know when his Soule is thus
contented? this frame of heart difcovers it felfe in
three particular acts, or paffages.

Wherein this   Firft, You may remember, that I told you before,
contentedneffe   that the finner was refolved to yeeld to God, and to
confifts.   fubmit himfelfe to his power, and pleafure, and hee
did begge mercy. Now the Soule that is truely aba-
                                                      fed,

fed, (though he feeke mercy) yet he feeth fo much
corruption, and unworthineffe in himfelfe, that hee
acknowledgeth himfelfe unfit for mercy. He cannot
avoyd the wrath of God, neither can he beare it,
therefore he faith, Oh mercy, mercy Lord! What
(faith the Lord) I had thought your owne duties,
and prayers, would have carried you out againft my
Juftice, and have purchafed mercy? Oh no (faith
the Soule) it is onely mercy that muft relieve and
fuccour me, but fuch is my vileneffe, that I am not
fit for the leaft mercy and favour; and fuch is the
wickedneffe of this wretched heart of mine, that
whatfoever are the greateft plagues, I am worthy of
them all, though never fo infupportable: and all the
Judgements that God hath threatned, and prepared
for the devill and his angels, they are all due to this
wretched Soule of mine, for I am a devill in truth;
onely here is the difference, I am not yet in hell: and
oh (faith the Soule) had the devils the like hopes,
and meanes, and patience that I have enjoyed, for
ought I know, they would have beene better than I
am. It is that which fhames the Soule in all his for-
rowes, and makes him fay, had they the like mercy?
Oh thofe fweete comforts, and thofe precious pro-
mifes that I have had, and that the Lord Jefus hath
made to mee, and hath come fo many heavie jour-
neyes to knocke at my heart, and fayd, Come to mee
ye rebellious children, turne ye, turne yee; why
will ye dye. Oh that mercy, that hath followed
me from my houfe to my walke, and there mercy
hath conferred with me, and from thence to my
clofet; and there mercy hath woed me: and in my
night

night thoughts when I awaked, there mercy kneeled
downe before me, and besought me to renounce
my base courses, yet I refused mercy, and would
needes have my owne will; had the Devills but such
hopes, and such offers of mercy, they that now
tremble for want of mercy; they would have given
entertainement to it; for ought I know : And what,
doe I seeke for mercy? shall I talke of mercy? Alas,
shall I seeke for mercy, when in the meane time, I
have thus slighted and despised it: what, I mercy?
the least of Gods mercies are too good for me, and
the heaviest of Gods plagues are too little for mee.
Nay, the soule findes no end in pleading, and therefore he reasons thus with himselfe, and saith, that
God cannot doe more against him than hee hath deserved; but be sure, he thinkes that God will not lay
more upon him than hee is worthy of. Nay, it is
sure the Soule cannot beare nor suffer so much, as he
hath deserved and pluckt upon himselfe, if God
should proceede in rigour with him. For the sinner
that will deale plainely, and discernes his evill exactly; it is easie for him to number up all his abhominations, and the soule thus reasons with it selfe,
and saith, I onely deserve eternall condemnation;
for the wages of all sinne is death, being committed
against an infinite Majestie, and against a Divine Justice, and then what doe all these my sinnes deserve,
committed, and continued in, and maintained against
the light of Gods Word, against all corrections, and
all checkes of conscience, and all the Commandements of God, hell is too good, and ten thousand
hells is too little to torment such a wretch as I am. In
truth,

truth, I begged mercy, but what, I mercy? I am aſhamed to expect it, and with what heart can I beg this mercy which I have troden under my feete? Shall that blood of Chriſt purge my heart, that bloud that I have trampled under my feete, and accounted it as an unholy thing? and when the Lord hath wooed me, and his wounds were bleeding, and his ſides goared, and his hideous cries comming into mine eares, *My God, my God, why haſt thou forſaken me*, yet this Chriſt have I ſlighted, and made nothing of his bloud, and can the bloud of Chriſt doe me any ſervice? indeed I doe crave grace, but how doe I thinke to receive any. All the pillars of the Church can teſtifie, how often grace, and mercy have beene offered to me, but I have refuſed it, therefore how can I begge any grace? And as the Text ſaith, *They ſhall ſee their ſinne and acknowledge their wayes, and judge themſelves worthy to be condemned.* So the Soule confeſſeth, that it is worthy of nothing that is good; it is not worthy of Gods love, nor of Gods preſervation, or any other priviledge, onely he confeſſeth that he doth loath himſelfe, and ſaith, Oh this ſtubbornneſſe, and villanie, and this wretchedneſſe of mine : what, I mercy? no, I am not worthy of any, it is more than I expect, I am onely worthy to be caſt out for ever. As the Prophet *Ezechiel* ſaith, *That thou mayeſt remember, and bee confounded, and never open thy mouth more becauſe of thy ſhame;* that is, they ſhall remember the evill that they have committed, and the Lords kindneſſe and merciethat they have oppoſed, and they ſhall be confounded, and not open their mouthes any more. So;

Ezech. 16. 63.

ROW.

now his tongue cleaves to the roofe of his mouth, and he faith, I remember my evill, and am afhamed to expect any mercy, I fought for mercy before, but now I fee I am unworthy of any, and worthy of all the judgements that God can powre upon me. The Soule confeffeth clearely, that hee hath deferved more than God will lay upon him; for if God fhould powre all his wrath upon him, he muft make him infinite to beare his infinite wrath, and therefore the Lord onely layes fo much upon him as he is capable of.

Secondly, the Soule acknowledgeth the equalnes of Gods dealings be they never fo harfh in this kind. He confeffeth that he is as clay in the hands of the Potter, and the Lord may deale with him as he will. Yea, the Soule is driven to an amazement at the Lords patience, that he hath beene pleafed to reprive him fo long, and that God hath not caft him out of his prefence, and fent him downe to hell long agoe. It is the frame of Spirit that the poore lamenting Church had, *It is the Lords mercy that we are not confounded, becaufe his compaffions faile not.* When a poore drunkard feeth how hee hath roared in the Alehoufe againft God and his truth, and how hee hath plotted againft the Saints, he wonders that ever God could beare with fuch a wretch, and that the earth hath not fwallowed him up quicke. And when the Lord hath humbled the heart of an adulterer, or adulterefle, he begins to thinke thus with himfelfe, the Lord faw all the evils that I have committed, and all my plottings, and all my inveiglings and allurings to this finne, and my delight in it : then
the

2.

Lament.3. 22.

the Soule admires that ever Gods Iustice was able
to beare with such a monster, and that God did not
confound him in his burning lusts, and cast him
downe to hell. Oh (saith he) it is because his mercies faile not, that my life, and all hath not failed
long agoe. Nay, the Soule concludes, that the Lord
should not save him. As *Nehemiah* saith, *Howbeit,* Nehem. 9. 38.
*thou art just in all that is brought upon us, for thou hast
done right, but we have done wickedly,* as if hee had
sayd, It is righteous that every man should lye under
his owne load, and therefore thou mayst justly condemne us. Nay, the Soule saith, That God cannot
but plague him for ought that he perceives in Iustice;
as *Daniel* saith, *Therefore hath the Lord watched upon* Dan. 9. 14.
*the evill, and brought it upon us, for the Lord our God
is righteous in all his workes which he doth, because we
obeyed not his voyce:* Hee speakes there of the 70.
yeares captivitie. So the Soule saith, Because the
Lord is just, and righteous, and doth not onely punish, but he cannot but punish, and therefore he justifies the Lord in all the plagues that ever can bee
inflicted upon him. And hence it is that the Soule
will not maintaine any kinde of murmuring or heart
rising against the Lords dealing, much lesse doth he
hide it in the Lord. But, though nature and corruption will be stirring, and sometimes the heart will be
grudging against the Lord and say, Why doth the
Lord thus, and why are not my prayers answered,
such a Soule is humbled, and such a Soule is comforted, and why not I as well as he, yet when any
such matter ariseth in the heart, he stifles, crusheth
and chokes these wretched distempers, and doth

O　　　　　　abase

abase it selfe before the Lord, saying, *What if God will not* (as the Apostle saith) speaking of the rejection of some, & the receiving of others: so the Soule saith, What if God will not heare my prayers? and what if God will not pacifie my conscience? nor shew any mercy to mee, I have my owne, and doth the Lord doe me any wrong, vile hell-hound that I am, I have my sinne and my shame, wrath is my portion, and hell is my place, I may goe thither when I will, it is mercy that God deales thus with me. Now the Soule comes to cleare God in all his providence, and saith, It is just with God that all the prayers which come from this filthy heart of mine, should be abhorred, and that all my labours in holy duties should never be blessed, for I have had these ends, and by-respects in all my duties; it is I that have sinned against checks of conscience, & against knowledge; and therefore it is just that I should carry this horrour of heart with me to my grave; it is I that have abused mercy, and therefore it is just and righteous with God, that I should goe with a tormenting conscience downe to hell; Oh that (if I be in hell) I might have a Spirit to glorifie and justifie thy Name there, and say, Now I am come downe to hell amongst you damned creatures, but the Lord is righteous and blessed for ever in all his dealings, and I am justly condemned.

Thirdly, Hence the Soule comes to be quiet and framable under the heavy hand of God in that helplesse condition wherein he is, so that the Soule having beene thus framed aforehand, it comes to this, that it takes the blow and lies under the burthen

and

and goes away quietly and patiently, he is quiet and
faith not a word more: oh! this is a heart worth gold
He accounts Gods dealing and Gods way to be the
fittest and most seasonable of all. Oh (saith he) it is fit
that God should glorifie himselfe though I be damned for ever, for I deserve the worst; whatsoever I
have it is the reward of my owne workes, and the
end of my owne way: if I be damned, I may thank
my pride, my stubbornnesse, my peevishnesse of spirit, and all my base corruptions; What shall I repine
against the Lord, because his wrath and his displeasure lies heavie upon me? let me repine against my
sin that made him to do it; Let me grudg against my
base heart that hath nourished these adders in my
bosome, shall I be unquiet and murmure against the
Lord, because this horrour of heart doth vexe me?
oh, no, let me blesse the Lord and not speake one
word against him, but let me repine against my sin,
as the holy Prophet *David* faith, *I held my tongue* Psal. 39.9.
*and spake nothing, because thou Lord haddest done
it.* So the soule faith, when the sentence of condemnation is even seazing upon him, and God seemes to
cast him out of his favour, then he faith, I confesse
God is just, & therefore I blesse his Name, and yeild
to him: but sin is the worker of all this misery that
hath befallen me. The holy Prophet *Ieremie* pleading of the great extremitie that had befallen the
people of God, faith, *woe is me for my hurt, my wound* Ier. 10. 19.
*is grievous, but I fayd, truely this is my griefe and I
must beare it.* This is the frame of a heart that is truely humbled; it is content to take al to it self and so to
be quiet, faying, this is my wound and I must beare

it, this is my forrow and I will fuffer it; thus you fee what the behaviour of the heart is in this contented-nes. Hold thefe well for they are of marvellous difficulty and great ufe. But, what is the dealing of the Lord that the foule muft be contented with?

Queſt.

Anſwer.

The behaviour of the Lord towards the Soule in this kind difcovers it felfe in two things. Fiſt, In what he will doe to the Soule. Secondly, in the manner of his dealing, how he will deale with the Soule, and the heart muft be contented with both thefe. Sometimes a man will beare a thing, but not the manner of it, that kills him; but God will make a finner waite upon him for mercy, and beg againe, and againe, and be content with the harfheft of his dealings, and glad he may have it fo too.

The firſt thing that God will have the Soule contented with.

The firft thing that God wil doe to the Soule, and which the Soule muft be contented with, is that falvation, and happines, and the acceptation of a mans perfon now muft be no more in a mans owne hands, nor in his owne abilitie, the Lord hath taken the ſtaffe out of his hand; and Salvation muft bee no more put in his owne power. Here is a wonderfull height of pride expreft before the Soule will yeeld to this. When *Adam* was created in his innocencie, the Lord put a faire ſtocke into his hand, and hee might have traded for himfelfe; and he had liberty of will, and power of grace, fo that he might have gotten the favour of God, by that which hee could do, if he wou'd have done that, he might have lived: But, when *Adam* had betrayed that truft which God committed o him in the ſtate of Paradife, becaufe he had forfeited this truft, the Lord tooke all away

from

from him, and nothing shall be in him, or from him
any more in the point of Iustification, or acceptation as any way meritorious. *Adam* in his innocency might have required mercy by vertue of a Covenant from God, but *Adam* shall now have nothing
in his owne power any more, but he shall have his
Iustification and acceptation (not in himselfe) but
in another, even Iesus Christ. So that the reason
why any Soule is justified and accepted with the
Lord, it is meerely in another, not in himselfe. It
is a great matter to bring the heart to this: for the
Soule to see nothing in himselfe, but all in and
through Christ; Oh this is a difficult worke. The
Lord will not trust him with a farthing token. There
are two passages marvellous usefull this way, and
therein you shall see the exceeding pride of a mans
heart, and it is very common. One passage is in the
Romans, Where the Text saith, *The Iew and the* Rom. 9.31,32.
Gentile sought for righteousnesse, that is, *how they*
might finde acceptance and righteousnesse in the sight
of God. The Iew sought this by the workes of the
Law, that is, by himselfe, by his sacrifices, and wash-
ings, and the like; and he thought these would have
acquitted him in the sight of God. But the Text
saith, *Israel which followed after the Law of righteous-*
nesse, hath not attained it, that is, they have not attained it, because they sought it not by faith, and from
Christ, but, in and of themselves, and therefore they
never came to attaine it. But most pregnant is that
other place, where the Apostle saith, *I beare them re-* Rom. 10.2,3.
cord that they have the zeale of God, but not according
to knowledge, for they being ignorant of Gods righteousnesse,

teoufneffe, and going about to eftablish their owne righteoufneffe, have not fubmitted themfelves to Gods righteoufneffe: the caufe why any man is acquitted of God; it is not becaufe of any thing that he hath or doth, but it is from anothers righteoufneffe. But what a great matter is this: The Text faith, *that going about to eftablish their owne righteoufneffe they have not fubmitted, &c*, here in this place there is this remarkeable. They thought to eftablish their owne righteoufneffe that is their owne duties, and fervices, their owne parts and abilities, and becaufe they thought to find acceptance for what they did, they did not fubmit. Submiffion argues a point of fubjection, and the want of this, horrible pride. This is marvellous devillish pride, that a man should fet up the lufts of his owne righteoufneffe, and duties, and thinke to finde acceptance, and reconciliation with, and pardon from the Lord becaufe of thefe. So that now the Soule is nothing, and the Lord faith unto him, thou shalt goe in ragges all thy dayes, that Chrift may be thy righteoufneffe. Thou shalt be a foole that Chrift may be thy wifedome; and thou shalt be weake, that Chrift may be all thy ftrength; and I will make thee fubmit to that righteoufneffe of Chrift. Nay, the Lord faith further, if you think to find acceptance, and to purchafe mercy by what you can doe, then come your way, and bring all thofe prayers, and duties, and fee if they can all anfwere my exact Law of righteoufneffe, and fatisfie my Iuftice. Thus the Lord is faine to emptie a man of himfelfe, this is an admirable work of the Spirit, when the heart is thus content to be at Gods carving,

carving and to have nothing of its owne, to be ignorant, weake, and meane, and to have all from a
Chrift. This is confiderable, every man would faine
bring fomething with him, even where God hath
wrought grace, and when we are all dead in the neft,
and all amort when we find it not, and we are ready
to fay, if I had thefe, and thefe enlargements, then
God would accept me, but becaufe I have not, the
Lord will reject me. What is that but to fet up the
merits of a mans parts and duties: therefore it is that
the Lord will bring the Soule to this, to be content
to bee juftified, (not for what hee hath,) but for
fomething in another, befides what he can doe to
entitle himfelf to heaven and happineffe. Therefore
the Apoftle faith, *To him that worketh not, but belee-* Rom. 4 5.
veth (on him that juftifieth the ungodly) *is faith ac-*
counted for righteoufneffe. This is our nature; We
would faine be Ioynt-purchafers with Chrift, and
have fomething of our owne of merit (to make us
find acceptance with God) as well as Iefus Chrift
in the point of Iuftification. But the Lord will bring
the heart to this, it fhal come as an ungodly wretched traitor, that the Lord may Iuftifie him in Chrift.
Why dare not a poore finner fometimes come to
Chrift, and looke to him for mercy; Oh, he is not
worthy. But, art thou not content to fee thy unworthineffe? Yes (faith he) but I fee fuch pride,
fuch litherneffe in holy duties, and fuch corruption
that I dare not goe to Chrift for mercy. If this bee
a burthen to thee, and if thou art content to be rid
of this, then Chrift hath prepared mercy for thee,
and thou mayft take it; the Lord will make thee
know

know that thou art not accepted, becauſe thou art worthy, but through Chriſt. The Lord juſtifies the ungodly.

The ſecond part of the Lords diſpoſe, that hee brings the Soule unto, it is this. As the Soule muſt looke for what it hath from another : ſo in the ſecond place, it muſt be content to take, what mercy, and what another will give. Not, what the Soule thinkes fitting; but, what mercy accounts the beſt for him. Now, ſee this bleſſed frame of heart in theſe three particulars.

The ſecond thing that the Soule muſt be content with.

Firſt, the Soule is content that mery ſhall deny what it will to the Soule, and the Soule is content, and calmed with whatſoever mercy denyes. If the Lord will not heare his prayers, and if the Lord will caſt him away, becauſe he hath caſt away the Lords kindneſſe, and if the Lord will leave him in that miſerable and damnable condition, which he hath brought himſelfe into, by the ſtubborneſſe of his heart, the Soule is quiet. Though I confeſſe, it is harſh and tedious, and long it is ere the Soule be thus framed; yet the heart truely abaſed, is content to beare the eſtate of damnation : becauſe he hath brought this miſery and damnation upon himſelfe. In a word, the Soule ſeeth, that it deſerves nothing at Gods hands; and therefore he is content, if God deny him any thing; and it befalls the Soule in this caſe as it did *David* : See how willingly hee takes, whatſoever the Lord ſhall allow him. Where hee ſaith; *Carry backe the Arke of God into the Citie, if I ſhall finde favour in the eyes of the Lord, he will bring me againe, and ſhew me both it and his habitation; but*

1 Sam.15.25, 26.

if

if hee shall say, I have no delight in *David, Behold, here I am, let him doe whatsoever is good in his eyes.* As it was with *David* for a Temporall Kingdome; So it is with the Soule for a Spirituall Mercy. The Soule saith, if there be any mercy for a poore rebellious creature, the Lord may looke gracioufly upon me; but if the Lord shall say, thou hast brought damnation to thy selfe, therefore I will leave thee in it. Behold, here I am, let the Lord doe with mee what he will.

But, some may here object and say, Must the *Object.* Soule, can the Soule, or ought it to be thus content, to be left in this damnable condition?

For the answere hereof; Know, that this conten-*Answer.* tednesse implies two things, and it may be taken in a double sense.

First, Contentednesse sometimes implies nothing elfe, but a carnall securitie; and a regardlesnesse of a mans estate, he regards not his owne soule, what he is, nor what he hath, nor what shall become of him. This is a most curfed sinne, and this contentednesse is nothing elfe, but a marvellous negligence, either of Gods glory or his owne good; and it is a sinne to give way to it; and it is a fore-runner of damnation to that man which entertaines it. The Soule that is truely humbled and abased, cannot (nay it dare not) say so in cold bloud, setting aside passions, and temptations.) Nay, this contentednesse argues damnation for ever. This is not meant in this place, neither is it lawfull to give way to it; and it is certaine, upon these termes the Soule shall never bee saved; God will make him

P   prize

prize mercy, and care for it too before he have it.

But then; Secondly, it implies a calmeneſſe of Soule not murmuring againſt the Lords diſpenſation towards him, and this contentednſſe is ever accompanied with the ſight of a mans ſinne, and the following of God for mercy. The ſoule that is thus contented to be at Gods diſpoſing, it is ever improving all meanes, and helpes that may bring him neerer to God, but if mercy ſhall deny it, the ſoule is ſatisfied and reſts well apaid, this every ſoule that is truly humbled may have, and hath in ſome meaſure. Yet you muſt not throw all at ſixe and ſeavens, no, it is a curſed diſtemper of ſpirit that you muſt hate as hell it ſelf. But this contentedneſſe is oppoſed againſt quarrelling with the Almighty, and this every humbled ſoule doth attaine unto, though it be not ſo plainely ſeene. As it is with ſome theefe that is taken for a robbery, and the ſentence of death hath paſt againſt him: he ſhould not neglect the uſing of means for to ſave his life and to get a pardon; and yet if he cannot get a pardon, he muſt not murmure againſt the Iudge for condemning of him becauſe he hath done nothing but Law. This theefe ſhould uſe means for a pardon; but if he cannot get one, he ſhould be contented though the ſentence paſſe againſt him So we ſhould not be careleſſe in uſing all meanes for our good, but ſtill ſeeke to God for mercie; yet thus we muſt be, and thus we ought to be contented with whatſoever mercy ſhall deny, becauſe wee are not worthy of any favour, and the humble ſoule reaſons thus with it ſelfe, and ſaith, my owne ſinne, and my abhominations have brought me into this damnable

ble condition wherein I am, & I have neglected that
mercy which might have brought me from it, therefore why should I murmure against mercy, though
it deny me mercie? and if mercy leave mee in that
miserable estate, which I have brought my selfe into, I have but the reward of my own workes. Marke
this well. He that is not willing to acknowledge the
freenesse of the course of mercy, is not worthy, nay,
he is not fit to receive any mercy: but that Soule
which is not content that mercy deny him what it
will; he doth not give way to the freenesse of the
Lords grace and mercy, and therefore that Soule is
not fit for mercy. I conclude all thus. Iudge with
your selves whether this be not a marvellous hideous pride of heart, or no? that the sinner, doth murmure because the Lord will not dispence of mercy
as he will himselfe, either the sinner thinkes that he
hath deserved mercy, and therefore he is angry with
God because he gives it not, or else he thinkes himselfe wiser to dispose of mercy than God; both
which are most devillish pride of heart, and arguments of a haughty heart that is not yet fit for mercy, nay, if this be in the heart, and if the heart allow of this, and continue in this distemper, the soule
cannot receive mercy.

   But some may object. Can a man feele this frame
of heart, to be content, that mercy should have him
in hell? doe the Saints of God finde this? and can
any man know this in his heart?

   To this I answer. Many of Gods servants have
beene driven to this, and have attained to it, and have
layd open the simplicitie of their soules, in being

con-

A Sillogisme.

Object. 2.

Answer.

content with this. But the secret paſſage of the Soule
is moſt ſubtle here, and hard it is to finde this, and
clearely to diſcerne this frame of ſpirit this way:
but the beſt way to gueſſe it, and to be able to diſcerne it, is this. For this end, you muſt know theſe
three things.

Firſt, that the Soule out of the nature of it, and
in nature cannot but deſire preſervation of it
ſelfe, and it is a rule that God hath ſtamped in the
creature, and therefore we muſt not thinke that nature muſt or ſhould, or can goe further then nature,
and it is not the fault of nature, that it is carried in
this kind.

But Secondly, the Soule being humbled, cannot
but yeeld it ſelfe, to be diſpoſed of by the Lord as
he will, yea, if the Lord will bring deſtruction upon it.

Thirdly, though the Soule ſometimes finde a ſecret rebelling againſt God, and a grudging againſt
the Lords dealings, & the ſinner begins to ſay, theſe
are my corruptions, and ſtill my ſinnes prevaile
againſt mee, and I ſhall one day periſh, and the
Lord ſeemes not to looke at me, and with that the
Soule ſometimes grudgeth, and repines at the providence of God, yet the heart that is truly humbled,
grudgeth at himſelfe, becauſe he hath ſuch a quarrelling heart againſt the Lords dealing with him in
this kind. Nay, I have knowne many in the anguiſh
of heart, when they have thus quarrelled with the
Almighty, they have falne into a deſperate extremity, and thought they had committed that ſinne
againſt the holy Ghoſt; inſomuch, that it hath made
them

them to walke more humbly before God all their dayes; but (I say) when the Soule findes these distempers, it labours to undermine them, and it dares not quarrell against God, it dare not but yeeld, and this is an argument that the Soule is content.

Secondly, the Soule that is contented comes to be well apay'd with this, that mercy shall take away from him what it will, friends, and meanes, and ease, and libertie, and credit, and whatsoever it is that the heart hath loved most. It is content that God should strip him naked of all: And hence it is, that we shall observe it in experience, and in practice. A broken battered Soule, that hath beene long overwhelmed with the weight of his corruptions, the Lord brings him to a marvellous desperate low ebbe: You may see a man sometime in the torment of Conscience, that nature and naturall parts begin to decay, his understanding growes weake, and his memorie failes him, and he growes to be marveloufly distracted, and besides himselfe; so that the party which was (before) a man of great, rich, and of able parts, and was admired, and wondred at for his wisedome, and government; he is now accounted a silly sot, and a mad man, in regard of the horor of heart that hath possesst'd him, in so much that the husband saith, Oh my wife is undone; and the father saith, my childe is undone, he was a fine witty child before, but now he is a very sot. Yea, the mercy of God will not leave a man before he be content to bee a despised man, that he may finde mercy and be saved, and mercy will plucke away all those parts and gifts from him, and make him glad to have salvation, and

all

all in another: And in conclusion, when God cheers
up his heart againe, he is more wise than ever, and
more able than ever, both for temporall, and spirituall affaires. *How can you beleeve* (saith our Saviour) *that seeke honour one of another.* Without
this dealing of God, no man would ever come to
heaven, though the Lord sometimes abates some
measure of it. It may be before this worke, the
Soule saith if I may have honours and ease, and libertie, and credit, so it is; I care not whether ever
I have drop of mercy or no: But the text saith, *How
can you beleeve which seeke honour one of another, and
not that honour which comes from God only.* Mercy will
bring you downe upon your knees, and you shall
not be content with the honours of the world, No,
no, mercy will make you content to be fooles, and
to take that honour onely which is from God,
though you be abased, and hated, and persecuted in
the world. It is against reason that the Soule can
beleeve, except this be in the heart.

A humble
Soule is con-
tent that mer-
cy shall rule
him.

   As the humbled Soule is content, that mercy shall
deny him any thing, and take any thing from him,
so it is content, that mercy enjoyne what it will, and
make what Edicts, and Lawes it will: So that the
Commands, and Precepts of the mercy of God in
Christ may take place in his heart. When *Iohn Baptist* came to prepare them for Christ, and the hearts
of the people were humbled, the *Publicans* came to
him saying, *Master, what shall we doe?* and so the soul-
deirs said, *Master, what shall we doe?* and he sayd, *Doe
no man wrong, but be content with your wages.* The
question is not now, covetousnesse, and cruelty,
                                                    What

Ioh.5.44.

Luke 3.13; 14.

What shall we doe? No, the souldiers came now, and sayd, thou art our Master, the Spirit of God, and the Spirit of wisedome is revealed to thee in the Word, command and enjoine thou what thou wilt, and they are content, with whatsoever hee commands them. The humbled heart is content, that mercy doe what it will with him, not onely that mercy shall save him, for so farre a reprobate, and a carnall hyppocrite may be content. The hypocrite is marvellous willing, that mercy shall save him, but his lusts and corruptions must rule him still. You are content that mercy should save you from your peevish heart, and yet your peevish heart must rule you still; and you are content that Christ should save you from your drunkennesse, and prophaning of the Lords Day, but these lusts must rule you still. A drunkard that hath gotten some dangerous surfeit, is content that the Physitian should cure him, not because he would leave his drunkennesse, but because he would have his health, and therefore being up, he returnes to his drunkennesse againe. And the theefe that is condemned to die, cryes for a pardon, not because hee would live to be an honest man, but to be free from the halter; and therefore when he is freed, he goes to the hye way and robs againe; it is not for honesty that he desires a pardon, but for libertie. Deceive not your selves: mercy will never save you, except mercy may rule you too. Here is a heart worth gold, and the Lord delights in such a soule, that falls into the armes of mercie, and is content to take all from mercy, and bee at mercies disposing, and to have mercy sanctifie him,

and

and correct him, and teach him, and to rule in him in all things. This the heart of a truely abased sinner will have, and it will say, good Lord doe what thou wilt with me; rule this soule, and take possession of me; onely doe good to the Soule of a poore sinner. If the Lord give any thing, he is content, and if the Lord take away any thing, or command any thing, he is content. You that are ruled by your lusts, think of this. When the Lord hath awakened and arrested your Soules, you are going downe to hell, Oh, then you will cry, Lord forgive this and that sinne; it is true, I have hated, and loathed the Saints of God, good Lord forgive this sinne, oh that mercy would save me, then mercy will answere, and say, When you are out of your beds, you will returne to your old courses againe; no, he that ruled in you, let him save and succour you: I will save none (saith mercy) except I may rule them too.

3.

Thirdly, the last degree of contentednesse is this. The Soule is willing that the Lord should make it able to take what mercy will give. This is a lower pegge that the Soule is brought unto. The sinner before had nothing of his owne in possession, nay, he can challenge nothing of the other, but meerely to doe what he will, and he is not able to take what mercy will give and bestow. And therefore he is not onely content that mercy provide what it thinks good, but also to give him strength to take what mercy gives. The beggar that comes to the dole, though he hath no meanes to helpe himselt withall, and though he can challenge nothing of the man, yet he hath a hand, and can receive the dole that is

given

given him, but a poore sinner is brought to this low ebbe, (and this shewes the emptinesse of it) that as he hath no spirituall good at all, and can challenge no good, neither is he able to take that good which mercy provides. The hand of the Soule whereby it must receive mercie, is faith, and the humbled soule seeth that he is as able to satisfie for his sinne, as to beleeve in a Saviour that must satisfie. And he is as able to keepe the Law, as to beleeve in him that hath fulfill'd the Law for him. In Saint *Iohn, beleeving is* Ioh. 1. 15. *called receiving,* and therefore the poore sinner seeth that it is not only mercy, and salvation that must do him good, but he seeth that if mercy and Salvation were layd downe upon the naile for beleeving and receiving of it, he could not doe it of himselfe, and therefore the Lord must give him a hand to receive it with. You know the Apostle *Paul* saith, *The na-* Phil. 1. 29. *turall man cannot receive the things that be of God.* And the same Apostle is plaine, *to you it is given to be-leeve.* So that faith is a gift, and a poore sinner is as able to create a world, as to receive mercy of himselfe. The want of this, is the cause why many a man that hath made good progresse in the way of happinesse, falls short of his hopes. Many a sinner hath beene awaked, and his heart humbled, and the Soule comes to heare of Christ, and thinks to lay hold of mercy, and Christ out of his owne proper power, and thus he deceives himself, and the faith that he dreamed to have, was nothing else but a fancie, a faith of his own framing; it was never framed by the Almighty Spirit of the Lord in heaven, he never saw need of the power of God, to make

Q   him

him able to believe as well as to save him, and there-fore his faith and all came to just nothing. Now the broken hearted sinner saith, All that I expect it must be from another, and I am content to take what mercy will give; and that mercy shall deny me what it will, and give me what it will, and I am con-tent that mercy rule in me, nay, that mercy must give me a heart to beleeve and to ake mercy, or else I shall never beleeve, Now you see what it is that the Soule must be contented withall.

The manner of Gods dea-ling.

Now I come to shew the manner of Gods dealing with the Soule, for the Soule must be content with this too, as I told you before. The manner of Gods dealing may appeare in three particulars.

I. First, the Soule stoopes to the condition that the Lord will appoint, be it never so hard, & it is content to come to Gods termes, be they never so harsh and wearisome. As, sometimes when the soule finds that the heaviest hand of the Lord hath laine long upon him, & that the sharpest arrows of the venome of the displeasure of the Almighty stick deepest in him, and he finds the fiercenesse of Gods wrath burning in his heart, and *that all his sins which have bin sealed up in a bag*, as *Iob* saith, *they are all set in order before him*, and the wrath of the Lord (more heavie than any moun-taine) falls upon his back, (I say) when the poore sin-ner findes himselfe thus pursued after, in the fiercest and most terrible manner, the abased heart dare not flie away from God, nor repine against the Lord, but he layes downe meekely. 1. He will not flye away from God, for that is his pride, Nay, he dare not doe it. He will not go with *Saul* to the Witch of *Endor*, nor

Iob 14.17.

nor with *Judas* to a halter. When the Lord let *Judas* see that hee had betrayed innocent blood, and fill'd his heart with horrour, he did not goe to God and lye down under the harshest horror, but he went to a rope and hanged himselfe, and all through his pride, becaufe he was not content with the harsh dealing of God, though he leaped from the fire-pan into the fire, As the proverbe is. And likewife *Cain* went into the land of *Nod.* So, when the Lord hath awakened a poore creature, and after a good while, that a man would have thought he had gone on a good way in a Chriftian courfe, at laft when he findes that he is not able to beare the wrath of God, but more iniquitie comes in againft him, then hee flyes off from God, and fals from a Chriftian courfe, and goes to the Ale-houfe, or fome other bafe corufe, and fo hardens his confcience: but (I fay) the humble Soule dare not doe fo, but lyes at Gods foote-ftoole, and if it were the very bottome of the dregs of Gods wrath, and the very fire of hell, he is content to undergoe Gods dealing. He doth not queftion Gods dealing, and fay, others are not thus, and thus terrified, and why fhould I be fo? No, the Soule returnes all againft it felfe, and faith, why doe I talke of others? they have not fuch untoward, uncleane peevifh hearts as I have. The humble foule refolves with the Church in *Micah, I have finned* Mich.7.9. *and therefore I will beare the indignation of the Lord:* So the Soule faith, I have finned moft hainoufly, I know not their finne, but I know my own finne, and therefore I will beare the Lords wrath, though it be never fo unfupportable, and unfufferable; Lord give

Q 2   me

me a heart. That I may be able to beare it. When a
Malefactor comes to the Affises, he lookes for nothing but condemnation, and execution, if hee can
scape with burning in the hand, or branding in the
forehead, or shoulder, he is glad, and goes well a-
payd, and cryes, God save the King, because hee
thought he should have beene hanged: So it is with
an humble, and a selfe-denying sinner; When the
poore creature findes the heaviest of Gods indignation upon him, and such strange distempers, as if a
thousand devils were within him, the soule quiets it
selfe thus, and saith, Why do I thus fret? and wherefore am I thus perplexed? it is well that I scape thus:
I might have beene in hell this day, and blessed bee
God that it is no worse, that I am not in hell; I
might have beene roaring in hell, as thousands of
poore reprobates are, that have no more hope of
mercy; therefore I will beare whatsoever the Lord
layes upon me.

Secondly, as he is content with the hardest measure, so hee is content with the longest time. He is
content to stay for mercy, be it never so long. After
the poore soule hath his eies growing dim with waiting for mercy, his hands grow feeble, and his
tongue cleaves to the roofe of his mouth, and his
heart begins to sinke, and his Soule shakes within
him, with waiting for the mercy and goodnesse of
the Lord, and yet he findes no mercy, and hath no
Inkling of any favour, yet God lookes a farre off.
Yet his Soule is content with this. If a begger
should stay halfe a day for an almes it would grieve
him, though that be his pride. See what *Esay* saith,

I

I will waite upon the Lord that hath hid his face from
Jacob and I will looke for him. As if the poore sinner
did say, The Lord hath hid his face away, and turned his loving countenance from mee, yet I will
looke towards heaven, so long as I have an eye to
see, and a hand to lift up, I will yet looke to heaven
to the Lord that hath not (as yet) heard nor answered my prayers; the Lord may take his owne time,
it is manners for me to waite and stay Gods time:
Away therefore with that peevishnesse, and that
discontentednesse of soule, that when a poore sinner hath called, and cryed, and findes no answer, and
heares no newes from heaven, he secretly intends to
lay all aside; As if a man, lift a weight againe, and
againe, and seeth that it is too heavie for him, he lets
it alone. So many poore creatures are content to let
all alone and say; Why should I waite upon God
any more? I have prayed, and cryed thus long, and
finde no answere: why should I waite any longer?
How now? who shall have the worst of it? cannot
God have his glory without your payers? Why
should you waite? this is horrible pride of heart.
Why should you waite? Its no marvell, that you
should take such State to your selves? who must
waite then? Must the King waite, or the Subject?
The Master, or the Servant? The Iudge or the Traitor? Downe with that proud and sturdy heart of
yours. An humble Soule dare not doe so; hee is
content to waite for Gods mercy, and you will bee
brought to it too, before ever the Lord wil give you
any mercy. The humble soule saith thus, I have waited thus long, and the Lord seemes to be angry with

my

my perfon, and prayers, and all is blafted, yet I will
waite ftill; Nay, I am glad that I may waite: What,
waite upon the Lord Iefus Chrift, and mercy? Yes,
and glad you may. Kings and Princes have done it,
and bleffed are they that waite upon mercy. Nay,
the poore broken heart refolves thus, and faith, it I
lye and licke the duft all my dayes, and cry for mercy al my life long, if my laft words might be mercy,
mercy, it were well I might get mercy at my laft
gafpe : Oh, I bleffe God, that yet I live here, and
and that I am not in hell as thoufands are, that waite
for judgement and vengeance; bleffed be God, that
yet I may waite, till God looke upon me in goodneffe and mercy.

3.

    Laftly, when the Soule hath ftayed a long time,
it is content with the leaft pittance of mercy; he is
not like many proud beggars, that thinke much
when they have ftayed long, if they have but a farthing. Nay, if hee have but from hand to mouth,
It is all that he craves, and all that hee lookes for.
This is our nature; We would faine have fomething
to trade withall, but the Lord will keepe the ftocke
in his owne hand, and the foule is content to have it
fo. He comes fometimes and God will not heare,
and he goes away, and comes againe, and then goes
away fafting, and well contented too. See how the
poore Woman of *Canaan* did. She comes to beg
mercy of our Saviour, and he fayd, *It is not lawfull*
to caß the childrens bread to dogs, truth Lord (faith
fhe) I am as bad as thou canft call me, I yeeld all, I
am as vile a finfull poore creature as ever any was;
Yet Lord the dogs may eate the crummes that fall from
their

Mat. 15 26.

Verfe 27.

their Masters table. You know the Dog must stay till his Master comes in, and when he is come hee must stay till he sit downe, and then till he cut his meate, and hee must not have the meate from his trencher neither, when he hath stayed all this while, he hath nothing but the crums. So it is with a poore sinner; you must not thinke that God will bee at your becke: No, you must be content with the crums of mercy, and pity, and lye under the table til the Lord let the crums fall. The humbled Soule saith, Lord, let my condition be never so hard, doe what thou wilt with me, let the fire of thy wrath consume me here, onely recover me hereafter, and let me finde mercy, and if the time be never so long, if at last gaspe I may finde mercy I am content, and whatsoever thou givest, I blesse thy name for it. The soule doth not quarrell with the Almighty, and say, Why are not my graces increased? and why am not I thus, and thus comforted, and refreshed? Nay, it lyes, and looks for mercy, and if it have but a crum of mercy, it is comforted, and quieted for ever. Thus the heart is brought very low.

Why doth the Lord thus bring the heart under, *Reason.* is this necessary and requisite? Yes, it is without all question, not onely convenient, but very necessary that it should be so. And the reason is taken from the nature of the covenant of grace which requires this; and without which the covenant of grace could not be fitted for us. For the covenant of grace is this, Beleeve and live. The condition on our part is faith, and beleeving. Now faith is nothing else, but a going out of the Soule, to fetch all from another,

as

as having nothing of it felfe, and therefore this refting in our felves, will not ftand with the nature of
this covenant. Now were it fo, that wee were not
refolved to yeeld to, and to be guided by another, it
is certaine, we could not have our hearts enlarged to
goe to that other: by whofe wifedome, and providence, we would not be guided and difpofed. To be
in our felves, and out of our felves, to have power
in our felves, to difpofe of any thing belonging to
our fpirituall eftate, and to fetch all from another;
thefe are two contraries, and therefore cannot ftand
together. To have the difpenfation of life, and grace
in our owne hands to difpofe of it as we will, it utterly overthrowes the nature of this fecond Covenant of mercy and grace in Chrift. For (I pray you
obferve it) this I take to be the maine difference, between the fecond maine Covenant of grace, whereof the Apoftle difputes fo often; and the firft Covenant of workes; which he fo often confutes. The
firft Covenant is, to Doe and Live, This *Adam* had,
and if he had ftood ftill, he fhould not have needed
any Saviour: The fecond Covenant is, Beleeve, and
Live, that is, to live by another. Thefe two cannot
ftand together, in one and the fame Soule, at one
and the fame time. The fame foule that is faved by
the Covenant of Grace, cannot be faved alfo by the
Covenant of Workes. The Lord in the beginning,
put the ftuffe into *Adams* hand, and he had liberty,
to difpofe of Life and Salvation; by reafon of that
abilitie, and that principle of Grace that God had
given him; for he had perfect knowledge, and perfect holineffe, and righteoufneffe; and by the power
of

of these he had liberty, freely to pleafe God, and to keepe the Law, and to be blefled in fo doing, and if he had done that which he had power to doe, hee might have beene bleft for ever, and we all in him, but he loft it, and fo overthrew himfelfe, and all his pofteritie : Now we being thus falne in *Adam*, and being deprived of all that holineffe, and righteouf-neffe which *Adam* had; now the finner is neither able to fulfill the Law, and fo to purchafe mercy for himfelfe; nor to fatisfie for that which is done amiffe. A finner muft dye, and yet he cannot fatisfie in dying : he is dead in finnes and trefpaffes, and ha-ving loft all that abilitie which *Adam* had : there-fore the Soule muft goe out of it felfe; and fince it is fo, that nothing which he hath, or doth can fave him, he muft goe to another; that whatfoever is a-miffe, that other may fatisfie for it; and whatfoever mercy is needfull, he may purchafe it; and whatfo-ever is to be done, he may doe it. Now, what wee have done amiffe, Chrift hath fatisfied for it, and what we cannot doe, Chrift hath done it; he hath fulfilled all righteoufneffe. And hence it is, that thefe two are fo profeffedly oppofite the one to the other; the Law, and Faith. The firft *Adam*, and the fecond *Adam*. Confider a paffage or two. The Co-venant of Workes, and the Covenant of Grace, can-not ftand together in the point of Life and Garce; As the Apoftle faith, *If it be of grace, then it is no* Rom. 11.4. *more of workes, and if it be of workes, then it is no more of grace.* As if he had fayd, *If a man be faved by grace, then he cannot be faved by workes, and if he be faved by workes, then he cannot be faved by grace.* And in ano-

R ther

Rom.4.14.

ther place the same Apostle saith, *If they which are of the Law be heires, faith is made voyd, and the promise is of none effect.* If a man that thinkes to merit life by the Law, be an heire; what needeth faith, or the promise. For, it is the nature of faith, to goe out to Christ, and to receive all from him; now if I had enough in my selfe, I had no neede of Christ, and faith were made of none effect. *You are saved by* Ephes. 2.8: *grace through faith,* saith the Apostle, *and that not of your selves.* There S. *Paul* brings in a deniall, not only of sinne, but of workes; and saith, *You are not saved of your selves.* He doth not say, of your sinne; but, your selves; you, and your workes, and all must be renounced, and all that you are, and doe, as any way meritorious; and not to bee found in your selves, but in Christ, before ever you can receive mercy from Christ. So I dispute thus. There is none that will save us, Man nor Angel, and our workes will not; therefore we must goe to Christ, and if we goe to Christ for all, and expect all from him, then we must be content, to be guided by him in all. Now, let me propound this question: Either thou must be content, to be at the dispose of God, and mercy, or at whose dispose wilt thou be? If thou wilt have any thing else (besides mercy) to dispose of thee, thou makest that to be a Mediator to thee. But haply thou wouldest dispose of thy selfe, and dispose of mercy after thy owne minde? Yes, so I thought. It may be thou sayest, I will have grace, if I may dispose of it. Thus a proud heart would faine have it in his owne hands; but upon these termes thou never hadst: (nay, thou never shalt have)

have,) grace. Here is the winding of the Soule. Therefore many dare not venture their Salvation upon
Gods free favour. But they would have it in their
owne power, that they may receive it when they
will, that they may be drunke and take grace, and be
proud and prophane, and take grace when they will.
It is a fottifh delufion of men, that are deluded, and
blinded by the devill. But that the Soule (which
would have it thus) cannot have it upon thefe
termes; I thus reafon.

He that will have grace from his owne difpofe, fhall   Syllogifme.
never have grace, becaufe he hath none in his owne po-
wer to difpofe of :

But he that is not content to be at the difpofe of grace,
and to be at the difpenfation of Gods good pleafure for
mercy and grace, he would have it to be at his owne
difpofing.

And therefore he fhall (nay he never can) have grace.

In a word. Who muft difpofe of you? Your felves?
then you muft have that grace which you can difpofe of, and thats juft none at all. Grace is meerely
in Gods hands to difpofe of. Thus we have brought
the Soule to be fitly prepared for Chrift, and mercy,
and grace.

Now let us doe as travellers do, they fometimes   The fumme of
fit downe, to reckon how many miles they have   all this worke
gone. So let us enquire, what we have fpoken. You   of preparation.
know I mentioned two things, neceffary in this
worke of preparation for Chrift. Firft, Contrition.
And fecondly, Humiliation. Firft, God brings the
finner to a fight of himfelf and his fin; and makes him
to be infupportably burthened with the vileneffe of

it,

it, so that now the heart of a poore sinner, seeth an
absolute necessitie of a change, and therefore thinkes
thus with himselfe, if I rest thus, I shall never see
God with comfort. That's for Contrition. Now
he seeth that he must change, and hee is content to
change; and therefore, though he will no more bee
drunke, nor follow his old base practises, yet he begins to sherke for his owne comfort, and he useth all
the ordinances of God, to see what they can doe for
him, and he goes to himselfe, and his selfe sufficien-
cies, and finding no succour there, hee falls downe
before the Lord and begs mercy, and yet hee seeth
himselfe unworthy of mercy, without which hee
must perish. He hath nothing, and he can doe nothing to merit it; yet he is content, that God should
dispose of him as he thinkes good, onely (if it bee
possible) he prayes, that the Lord would shew mercy
to a poore forlorne creature Now the sinner is prepared, and fitted for Christ, as a graft for the stocke.
He is come to the very quicke, and is as little as may
be. All his swelling sufficiencie is pared away: For,
he is not onely brought to renounce his sinne, but
even his sufficiency, and all his parts and abilites;
which *Adam* needed not have done, if he had stood
in his innocencie. In a word, hee is wholly pluckt
from the first *Adam*, (for here is the maine lift.)
So that now the second *Adam* Christ Jesus, may
take possession of him, *and be all in all in him*, (as the
Apostle saith:) Now, the Soule is a fit matter for
Christ to worke upon, namely, to make him a vessell
fit to receive mercy and grace: and when hee hath
fitted him for mercy, he will give it to him: and
                                                    when

when he hath given him grace, he will maintaine it, and increase it, and then quicken it, and crowne it, and perfect it in the day of the Lord Jesus Christ. And lastly, he will glorifie himselfe in all these. Here is a right Christian indeed, that expresseth Christ in all. Christ preparing, Christ giving, Christ maintaining, and increasing, and Christ quickening, and Christ crowning. Thus you see that it is not left as a matter of liberty, but it is of necessitie required, that the heart bee thus contented: every humble heart hath this in some measure, though not (all) so sensibly.

The uses are double. First, to the people, to shew them what to doe. Secondly, to the Ministers.

Vses.

The uses for the people are. First, for instruction. Secondly, for Examination. Thirdly, for Terrour. Fourthly, for Exhortation.

The first Use is for instruction, and that is double. The first use

First, Is it so that the humble soule is content to to the people. be thus at the Lords disposing? then from hence we collect this use, that they which have greatest parts, gifts, meanes, places, abilities, and honors; for the most part they are most hardly brought home to the Lord Jesus Christ. They that are most hardly humbled, they are most hardly converted; how hard a thing is it for such men as have gifts, and learning, and wisedome, or any bignesse that makes them swell naturally, how hard is it (I say) for such men to be saved. I wish their courses did not testifie the same; they that are most high and greatest in gifts, and place, they must come in at the straite gate, and what a hard and difficult worke that is, judge

R 3   you

you, and therefore it is hard for them to come home to the Lord Jesus Christ, Humiliation is the emptiing of the soule from whatsoever it hath that makes it swell. The heart must not joy in any thing, nor rest upon any thing, but onely yeeld to the Lord Jesus Christ to be at his disposing and carving, now these parts and gifts, and abilities and meanes (both for judgement and place) they are great props and pillars for the heart of a carnall man to rest upon, and to quiet it selfe withall, and to looke for some good there-from; and when the heart is setled upon such pillars as these are, it is hard for the word of God to prevaile with that heart. The Prophet *Ieremie* knew it well enough, and therefore he said, *I will goe to the* Ieremy 5. 5. *rich and honorable, and they burst all bonds a sunder, and brake the yoke.* The poore were naught, but the rich were exceeding vile; and our Saviour proves it; for when the rich young man came to Christ & said, *Master, what shall I doe to have everlasting life?* Christ answered thus, go, sell all that thou hast, but he would not, and hereupon our Saviour comes to shew the difficultie of the worke of salvation, saying, *it is easier* Mat 16. 23. *for a Camell to goe through the eye of an needle, than for a rich man to enter into the kingdome of heaven.* It is true, a rich man may be brought home, but it is easier for a Camel, &c. There is great difficulty for a man that hath many gifts and parts to deny all, and to be at the Lords disposing. If a man were fit to cut a Camel so small till he were fit to goe through a needles eye, what a worke would it be: so it is with a great man. The blind Pharisees saw this when they sayd, Ioh. 7. 48. *doe any of the rulers beleeve in him?* as if they had sayd,

a

a company of Coblers, and Tailors, and the bafeſt
fort of people beleeve in him, it is they onely that
will not ſweare, and that will ſanctifie the Lords
Day; But doe any of the great men, and rulers beleeve. The Apoſtle alſo tooke it for confeſt, and
therefore he ſayd, Brethren you ſee your calling, *how*
not many wiſe men after the fleſh, not many mighty men,
not many noble men are called. Indeed, bleſſed be God, 1 Cor.1.26.
there are ſome great, ſome wiſe, and ſome noble
men converted. But, not many. For they have ſo
much of themſelves, that they are hardly brought
to renounce themſelves. Therfore commonly greatneſſe and wickedneſſe goe both together. And it is
a pretty ſpeech of the Prophet *David, There is that*
great Leviathan, that great Whale; little rivers have
their little fiſhes, but there is that *Leviathan.* So,
there is that hideous pride of ſpirit, and that ſtrange
reſiſtance of God and his grace; thoſe fearefull cry-
in ſinnes in great men. Yea, many mighty men, except God give them a great deale of grace, they are
peſtered with a great deale of corruption; Inſomuch
that they are hardly brought home. For a rich man
to become poore, and a noble man to be abaſed, and
for a wiſe man to be nothing in himſelfe, this will
coſt hot water, and yet it will be in all that belong
to the Lord. See what the Prophet *Eſay* ſaith, *The* Iſa.1 12.14.
day of the Lord of Hoſts ſhall be upon every one that is
proud and loftie, and upon every one that is lifted up,
and he ſhall be brought low, and upon all the Cedars of
Lebanon that are high and lifted up, and upon all the
Okes of Baſhan, and the glory of the Lord ſhall be exalted
in that day. As if he had ſayd, The Lord ſhall undermine

dermine the mountains, and make thofe tall Cedars
fit to come in at this ftrait gate. The poore receive
the Gofpel, and he that will have the pearle, muft
part with all that he hath; not that God will take
away all thofe outward things and parts, but that he
muft loofen his affection from thefe if he will have
Chrift. A poore creature that hath nothing, may
more eafily come to the price of the Lord Jefus
Chrift, then he that hath his hundreds, and thoufands a yeare : What (faith one) muft a man part
with all thefe? Yes, the Lord will have the love
that was fet upon thefe, wholly to himfelfe.

Right worfhipfull and beloved, and you of the
Miniftery, fuffer the words of Exhortation. The
greater your parts and abilities are, the greater is
your danger; and the greater your places are, the
more hard will it be for you to come home to the
Lord Jefus Chrift. Therefore as ever you defire
comfort to your felves? goe afide into your clofets,
and thinke thus with your felves, The Spirit faith,
Not many Noble men, not many mighty men, not ma-
ny wife men after the flefh are called. Hath the Lord
advanced me? then the more care I had neede have,
and the more I had neede to tugge and toyle for
Chrift, for it is marvellous hard to have this proud
heart humbled, and for an honorable man to lye and
licke the duft, and to take the crummes under the table. You that have thefe honours, and friends, and
means, and parts, for the Lords fake, let none of thefe
beare vp your hearts againft the truth of Chrift, and
let none of all thefe make you fwell, and fay, becaufe
I am great, or rich, or honourable, or wife, therefore

I

I muſt not be checked, and ſhall ſuch a man as I bee
at the command of a poore Miniſter? alas, we deſire
not to have you at our commands, onely we would
have you be content to be at the diſpoſe of the Lord
Ieſus Chriſt, and that you muſt be; if you belong to
him: and glad you may. It is obſervable that when
the Turke comes into the congregation, or the Temple of his Idoll, he layes by all his ſtate, and hath no
man to attend hir: for the while: ſo let every man
that hath riches, honours, and parts; let them be as if
they had none. You that are rich, be as if you had no
riches, and you that are honourable as if you had no
honors, and you that are wiſe, as if you had no wiſedome; when you come to heare the Word of God,
humble your ſelves, and ſay, my wiſedome, riches,
and depth of my judgement ſhall not hinder me, but
whatſoever it is that is my part and my portion, let
the Lord ſpeake to me, as if I were the meaneſt and
weakeſt in all the congregation. The Lord give you
hearts to do it, the worke is hard, and therefore put
hard to your hearts to doe it.

Secondly, is an humble Soule content to be at the The ſecond
Lords diſpoſe? then hence I collect that, an humble uſe for in-
heart makes all a mans life quiet, and marvello ſly ſtruction.
ſweetneth whatſoever eſtate he is in. That which
makes a man content in every condition muſt needs
make him quiet whatſoever eſtate he is in; howſoever the heart that is truly humbled may ſometimes
be toſſed and troubled, yet he is not diſtracted, becauſe he is contented, as it is with a ſhip upon the ſea
when the billowes begin to roare and the waves are
violent, if the Anchor be faſtned deepe, it ſtayes the

S ſhip;

ship; let the tempest be what it will: so this worke of humiliation is the Anchor of the soule; the world is the sea, the ship is a soule that is truly humbled, the deeper this humiliation is, the more quiet is the heart, and the more it is calmed. When *Iob* in the time of his extremity gave way a little to his proud and sturdie heart, he quarrelled with the Almighty, his friends and all, but when the Lord had humbled his proud heart, he said, *behold I am vile and base, once have I spoken, yea twice; but now no more.* And it is observed of *Ionah* that when he was in peace and in quietnesse, he had a sullen heart, and when the Lord said, *doß thou well to be angry?* yea (saith he) *I do well to be angry.* See how distracted, a distempered proud heart is; but take *Ionah* in the Whales belly, and we shall heare no more newes of quarrelling, but of praying, and there he abased himselfe; as it is with a Physitian, when the Patient hath some vehement fit of a Fever or the like; that he cannot sleepe, they use to give him a little *Opium* and that makes him rest a little. This humiliation of heart is like *Opium:* there are peevish fits of a proud heart that no word nor commandes will rule a man, but he must have what he will, or else he will set his mouth against heaven, but a little receipt of this *Opium* wil quiet al, if he could but come to see his own emptinesse and wretchednesse, and get his heart to be at Gods disposing, then his heart would be wonderfully calmed and meekened whatsoever he endured.

Iob. 40 4.

Three benefits of Humiliation

Humiliation gives quiet to a mans course in three causes. First in the fircest temptations; Secondly, in the heaviest oppositions of men. Thirdly, in the greatest

greatest povertie that can befall a man in this life.

In the strongest temptations. When Sathan begins to besiege the heart of a poore sinner, and layes battery against him; the Soule is so setled, that hee cannot be removed. See how the humbled heart tires the Devill, and runnes him out of breath, and out-shoots him in his owne Bow, in the very highest of all his malice and indignation. Take a poore Soule at the under, when he hath beene throughly burthened with a corruption, and layd gasping for a little grace, and favour, and could not finde any evidence of mercy; the Soule cryes continually, and begs for mercy earnestly; the devill seeth him, and (having some permission from God, so to doe) hee lets flye at the poore soule, and labours to knocke him off from his course, and saith to him in this manner.

Doest thou thinke to get mercy from the Lord? and doest thou dreame of any mercy at the hands of God? when thy own Conscience dogs thee. Nay goe to the place where thou livest, and to the chamber where thou lyest, and consider thy fearefull abominations, and how thou art foyled by them to this day, set thy heart at rest, God heares not, and respects not the prayers of such vile sinners. *Sathan objects.*

Now, the soule seeth this easily, and confesseth it plainly, and the humbled Soule saith, it is true. I have often denyed the Lord, when he hath called upon me, and therefore he may justly deny mee, yet seeke to him for mercy I must, and if the Lord will cast me away, and reject my prayers I am contented; if he doe cast mee away, what then Sathan? *The Soule answeres.*

Sathan. than : what then, saith the devill? I had thought this would have bin enough to make thee despaire. Yet this is not all : for God will give thee over, and leave thee to thy selfe, and to thy lusts and corruptions, and thy latter end shall be worse than thy beginning; and thou shalt call, and cry, and when thou hast done, be overthrowne; that loose, uncleane, and proud heart of thine will overthrow thee for ever, God will leave thee to thy selfe, and suffer thy corruptions to prevaile against thee, and thou shalt fall fearefully, to the wounding of thy conscience, to the grieving of the hearts of Gods people, to the scandall of the Gospell, and the reproach of thy owne person.

The Soule answers. Yet the humble Soule replies in this manner, and saith, if the Lord give mee up to my base lusts, which I have given my selfe so much liberty in, and if the Lord will leave mee to my sinnes; because I have left his gracious commands, and if I shall fall one day and be disgraced, and dishonoured, yet let the Lord be honoured, and let not God lose the praise of his power, and justice, and I am contented, if God doe leave me, what then Sathan?

The Devill objects. What then saith the devill? I had thought this had beene enough to drive thee out of thy wits, yet this is not all. For when God hath left thee to thy sinnes, then the Lord will breake out in vengeance against thee, and get praise from that proud heart of thine, and make thee an example of his heavie vengeance to all ages to come, and therefore it is best for thee to prevent an untimely Iudgement, by an untimely death.

The

The humble heart is quieted all this while, and replyes, whatſoever God can, or will doe I know not: yet, ſo great are my ſinnes, that he cannot, or (at leaſt) will not doe ſo much againſt mee, as I have deſerved; if the Lord doe come in Iudgement againſt mee I am contented; ſay what thou wilt, what then Sathan? Thus you may runne the devill out of breath; then the devill leaves the humbled Soule. The Soule anſwers.

The want of this Humiliation of heart, is it whereby men are brought to deſperate ſtands; ſo that ſometimes one man goes to a haltar, another runs out of his wits, and another drownes himſelfe: all this is horrible pride of heart. Why will you not beare the wrath of the Lord? It is true indeed, your ſinnes are great, and Gods wrath is heavie, yet God will doe you good by it; and therefore be quiet. In the time of warre, when the great Cannons flye off, the onely way to avoyd them, is to lye downe in a furrow, and ſo the Bullets flye over them, whereas they meete with the mountaines and tall Cedars. So it is with all the temptations of Sathan which beſiege us. Lye low, and be content to be at Gods diſpoſing, and all the temptations of the devill, ſhall not be able to diſquiet or diſtract thee.

Secondly, when Sathan is gone, then comes the troubles, and oppoſitions of the world. And this Humiliation of heart, gives a ſecret ſetling to the Soule, againſt all the railings, and oppoſitions of the wicked world: For, this takes off the unrulineſſe of the heart. So that when the Soule will not contend with oppoſitions, but is content to beare them, it is not The ſecond benefit.

not troubled with them. The humble Soule seeth,
God dispensing with all oppositions, and therefore
it is not troubled with them : A man is sometimes
Sea-sicke, not because of the Tempest, but because
of his full stomacke; and therefore, when he hath
emptied his stomacke, hee is well againe : So it is
with this Humiliation of heart. If the heart were
emptied truly, though a man were in a Sea of oppositions, if he have no more trouble in his stomack,
and in his proud heart, than in the oppositions of the
world, hee might be quieted. Consider *David*,
when he was in the wildernesse, and sent to *Nabal*
for some reliefe, see how he raged extreamly against
him, because he was denied it: The reason was not in
the offence, but in the pride of his heart. Take the
same man in the persecution of *Absalon*, and when
Shimei cursed him saying; Art thou not he that kild
such and such, and that committed adultery with the
Wife of *Vriah*, In this his heart was marveilous
quiet, and now he was able to beare it, better than
the souldiers that were with him. Though his cause
was just, and he might have revenged it : yet now
he was humble and brought under , and therefore
quieted though never so much opposed. This Humiliation of heart so settles a man, that though ten
thousand oppositions come against him, yet nothing
will disquiet him. Cast disgrace upon the humble
heart causelesly, & he cures it thus, he thinks worse
of himselfe than any man else can doe, and if they
would make him vile and loathsome, he is more
vile in his owne eyes than they can make him, and
therefore he is contented, If they imprison an humble

margin notes:
1 Sam. 25.12, 13.

2 Sam. 15,25.

2 Sam. 16.6.7. 8,9,10.11.12.

ble Soule, and persecute him, he wonders at Gods goodnesse, so farre hee is from being discontented, that he wonders at Gods goodnesse, and mercy towards him, that he would cast him into a Dungeon, when he might have cast him into hell.

Thirdly and lastly, this Humiliation of Soule, brings in satisfaction and contentednesse, in all the wants that may befall him. Take away from him what you will, and deny him any thing, yet he will be quiet. He that is contented with all Gods dealing towards him, cannot be disquieted with any thing; The humble soule justifies God, and is pacified, and joynes side with Gods provideuce, he justifies God in whatsoever he doth, and therfore is quiet in whatsoever he hath done. The ship that goes with wind and tide goes easily, but if it goes against wind and tide, it is wonderfully troubled; so, when the humble Soule goes on with Gods blessed providence, and goes that way which the will of God goes: he goes on quietly, and the want of this humiliation of heart is the cause of all your disquietnesse; when you will stand in opposition against the Almighty; the Lord will have you poore, and you will be rich, the Lord will have you base and meane in the world, and you would be honorable, the Lord on the one side, & you on the other side, you would have it, and the Lord saith you shall not; if all come not according to your minde, oh then you flye out, God must be of your mind, and be at your beck, and this you must have, and that you will have, or else God shall heare of you: thus you make your owne trouble, and this troublesome Spirit breeds all the

The third benefit.

for-

forrow that befalls you; whereas if you would goe
on with God, you might be quieted and comforted
whatſoever condition you were in; as one ſayd, that
he could have what he would of God; why, how
was that? becauſe, whatſoever Gods will was, that
was his will; humiliation quiets all, and ſupplyes
all wants, once make the good will of God that
which thy heart ſhall yeeld unto, and Gods providence the beſt that can befall thee, and then live
comfortably for ever. Oh! that our hearts were
brought to this. But the pride and vileneſſe of our
hearts is ſuch, that we trouble our ſelves needleſly:
therefore above all, labour for this. Be content to
want what God will deny, and to waite Gods good
pleaſure, and to bee at his diſpoſing, and then live
quietly, and comfortably for ever. Oh! that I could
bring your hearts to be in love, with this bleſſed
grace of God. Is it ſo, that Humiliation brings quiet
in all a mans conditions? Is there not a Soule here
that hath beene vexed with the temptations of Sathan, did you never know, what it is to be under the
malice of an enemie, and did your owne diſtempers
never trouble you? Have none of you found hard
meaſures at the hands of wicked men? is there never a Soule here that is burthened with many wants,
and that loves his owne comfort? have you not
many neceſſities at home, the want of friends, and
meanes, and even of common neceſſeries, and would
you arme and fence your ſelves, that no wants may
diſquiet you, nor trouble you, but in all, to be above
all, and to rejoyce in all; more then all oppoſitions
in the world can doe you hurt: then be humbled, and
for

for ever quieted. Whatſoever can or ſhall befall you,
by the devill and his inſtruments, and if every ſpire of
graſſe were a devill, be humbled, and then be above
all the devills in hell, and all temptations, and oppoſitions, that they ſhall not ſo diſquiet you, as to cauſe
you to be unſetled or uncomforted.

In the next place, you are to be deſired, to try The ſecond
your ſelves by the former truth : and let every man V ſe.
try his owne heart, whether ever God hath given
him this gracious diſpoſition of Soule or no? You
muſt come to this truth : for there is no juſtification
nor expectation without this ; Nay, there is no faith
can be infuſed into the ſoule, before the heart be
thus fitted and prepared : no preparation, no perfection. Never humbled, never exalted : therefore
let every man and woman, lay their hearts to the
former truth, and conſider this one thing in the generall. So farre as the heart is from this contended-
neſſe to be at Gods diſpoſe, ſo farre it is from true
preparation for Chriſt. You muſt be emptie, if ever
Chriſt fill you : you muſt be nothing, if you would
have Chriſt all in all to you. Thus much in the generall. But, now let us come to the particular trials : and herein let us conſider two things. Firſt, the
truth, and ſoundneſſe of our Humiliation. Secondly, the meaſure of it : both of theſe, this Doctrine
doth diſcover to us. It is very profitable to handle
them both, that they which have not this worke may
be humbled, and that they which have it, may ſee
how farre they come ſhort of the meaſure which
they ſhould and might have, the want of which is

the caufe of much forrow, and the want of much comfort.

How to try the truth of our Humiliation.

You may try the truth of this worke of humiliation, thus. In the generall, looke how you are difpofed of in your lives, and converfations. But in particular, that you may fee where wee be, let us obferve thefe three rules.

Firft, let us fee, what is it that fwayes our reafons, and judgements. Secondly, What is it that over-powers our hearts, our wills, and affections. Thirdly, What is it that rules our lives and converfations. Try your hearts by thefe rules, and then it will be plaine and cleare, whether you be truely humbled, and abafed or no. You know (I told you) that you muft not onely be difpofed off by God (for God will difpofe of you, whether you will or no, he will rule all things in heaven and earth, hee will either crufh thofe proud hearts of yours by Humiliation here, or elfe caft you downe to hell for ever,) but you muft be content to be at Gods difpofing. To beginne with the former; namely, to fee what fwayes our judgements: If you will attend, I hope you fhall know fomething in your owne hearts, you that are weake; as for the other, haply they come to quicken up their hearts, and to renew that which they knew before.

What fwayes our Reafons.

Firft, let us trie whether we fubmit in our judgements or no? Here is a maine breach; contrary to this fubmiffion is a mans carnall reafon, and that marvellous height of our conceits, when wee raife up our owne carnall reafon, as fo many holds,

and

and maintaine them againſt the truth of Chriſt ;
and whereſoever this frame of minde is, there this
worke of humiliation was never wrought. And
this is in too many. When a man ſwels in his owne
conceits againſt the truth of Chriſt. That's a ſweete
place to this end in the *Romans.* Where the Text
ſaith, *The wiſedome of the fleſh,* or as it is in the
Originall ; *The carnall minde is enmitie againſt God, for* Rom 8 7,
it is not ſubject to the Law of God, neither indeede can be.
The carnall mind, and all the reaſonings, and wiſedome of it, is not onely an enemy, but it it enmitie
againſt God. The Apoſtle doth not ſay, that a carnall mans wiſedome and reaſon doth not obey, but,
he is not able to beare the truth, he (as it were) ſets
himſelfe in battell array againſt it, it cannot be ſubject
to the Law of God. This is a maine wound in all the
ſonnes of *Adam,* That a man (as it were) deifies
himſelfe, and his owne dreames, and devices, and
makes his owne conceit, a line and levill to all his
converſation. So that the carnall minde, will bend
the truth to his minde though hee breake it. Here is
the marvellous pride of a mans mind. Hence it is
that the Apoſtle adviſeth us to *be wiſe with ſobrietie.* Rom.1 2.3.
As if hee had ſaid, a man may be drunke witth his
owne conceits ; as when a drunkard hath gotten his
braines well ſteeped in Wine and beare ; then whatſoever he conceits in his mind, muſt needs be as true
as Goſpell. So it is with a carnall minde. Though
arguments be never ſo plaine, and Scriptures never
ſo pregnant ; yet a carnall wretch will carry himſelfe
againſt all, and ſay, it is not my judgement, I am

not

not of that mind. This is the height of our mind, as if he did say, I doe not thinke it, let the word of God, and his Ministers say what they will to the contrary; they shall not perswade mee of it. Doest thou finde this in thy selfe, then it is an undoubted argument, thou never hadst a heart truely humbled.

1 Cor. 8. 2. See what the Apostle saith, *If a man thinkes that hee knowes any thing, hee knowes nothing as hee ought to doe.* You thinke you are as wise as you neede to be, and you are not children yet. You that thus lift and set up your selves in your owne concetis, whatsoever you be, you know nothing as you ought to doe. And therfore the Apostle spakes of some *that were puft up* Colloss. 2. 18. *in their owne conceits, intruding into those things which they have not seene, vainely puft up in their owne minds.* You conceive and imagine thus and thus, and will not beleeve the Minister of God whatsoever hee saith, therefore you are puft up, and this is not a heart truly humbled and kindely wrought upon.

A carnall man presseth into some imagination, as to his owne proper possession. As the old proverbe is: The foole will not leave his bable for all the Citie of *London.* So a carnall heart saith, I cannot be otherwise perswaded. I say, then the case is cleare, is it so with thy judgement and carnall reason ? then as yet thou wert never under the power of this truth, thou shottest up doores against Iesus Christ, he cannot come in to informe thee, thou art so full of thy selfe.

Objection. But some will say, how doth this carnall reasoning lift up it selfe against the truth of Jesus Christ ?

To

To this I anſwer, the lifting up of my carnall rea- *Anſwer.*
ſon, makes it ſelfe knowne in three particulars, and
by theſe you ſhall know when your conceits carry
you aloft from the truth of Chriſt.

Firſt, A carnall reaſon being thus puſt up, it is not
willing to know the Word of God, nor his truth, e-
ſpeciall thoſe truths that are troubleſome and tedious to him; preach and ſpeake what you will, but
preach not that. Hee either wiſhes himſelfe deafe
that he could not heare, or the Miniſter dumbe that
he could not deliver thoſe truths. The Lord ſent
the Prophet *Eſay* to preach to the people, and yet
to ſeale them downe to eternall deſtruction, and
therefore the Lord ſaith, *Goe tell this people, yee heare,* Eſa.6.9,10.
*but underſtand not ; ſee, but perceive not ; make the heart
of this people fat, they winke with their eyes.* As it is with
a bleare eye, that is not able to looke againſt the
Sunne, but ſhuts for feare the Sunne ſhould hurt it.
So, a carnall proud minde is not able to looke into
the truths that may trouble it, and that would a-
waken his bleare eye. And in another place, the
people doe intreate the Prophet *Eſay, to goe out of
the way, and to turne aſide out of that path ; cauſe the Ho-* Eſay 30.11.
ly one of Iſrael to ceaſe from before us. As if they
had ſaid, Wee cannot endure this holineſſe, we cannot brooke this exactneſſe, you bid us to be holy or
elſe God will deſtroy us, get you out of that path ;
they were weary of thoſe bleſſed truths. A double
example we have of this diſtemper of ſpirit in holy
Scriptures. As in *Iob, where the wicked ſay to God,*

depart

depart from us, for wee desire not the knowledge of thy wayes. The drunkard desires not to heare of any horror of his heart for sinne: and the hypocrite desires not to heare that he must be sound, and sincere, and keepe touch with God in every thing; and so all ungodly men goe against the truth of God, which crosseth their lusts and corruptions. And in *Timothy*, it was the range of a cursed distemper of spirit in a company of wretches of this age. The Text saith,

2 Tim. 4. 3. *The time shall come when they shall not endure sound doctrine.* And here it is to be noted, that a company of carnall Gentlemen, and base refuse people of other degrees are come to this passe, that let a plaine searching truth be discovered, they turne away from it, and cannot heare it with patience; but if any man will tell them some fine stories, Oh, this pleaseth them admirably: they cannot endure sound doctrine that searcheth the heart, and awakens the conscience, they cannot brooke that: now, an humble heart is of another mind, it is willing to heare any thing from the Lord, and any message from heaven; and the humble Soule saith, Speake on Lord, thy servant desires to heare: be the word never so troublesome, and the truth never so much crossing his lusts, hee is well content to heare it. Nay, he desires that especially, and hee is calmed with it. Marke what *Eli*

1 Sam. 3. 17. said, *Keepe not backe from me, but let mee heare whatsoever the Lord hath said unto thee.* An humble Soule comes to this passe, and saith, If there be any sinne, or any wickednesse in my heart, good Lord discover it,

it, and, if there be any duty to be done, Lord let me
know it. And as *Cornelius* said. *Wee are all here pre-* A&s 10.33.
sent before the Lord, to heare whatsoever thou art com-
manded of God. So the humble Soule saith, Whatsoever trouble it brings, I yeeld to the truth, and desire to heare it.

Thirdly, As the carnall reason shuts his eye, and
will not looke upon the truth, so in the second place,
if it be so, that it must heare that which it would not;
what is the next shift that it hath, bee will not suffer
himselfe to be convinced by the truth, but when the
truth comes in with plainenesse, and power, he labours what he can to gather up objections and ca-
vills against the truth, that he may oppose the power
of Gods Word, that sith it is so, that hee must heare
it, he labours to make it false. This is considerable.
Vnto them that are contentious, and doe not obey the Rom. 2.8.
truth, but obey unrighteousnesse shall be indignation and
wrath. Who are they that are contentious; not onely they that contend with their neighbours, but they
that contend against the truth, for so the words following doe import so much, *which obey not the*
truth. One man heares a close point, and then hee
goes away, and saith, I will not beleeve it, I know
Reason, and I will be bound to confute it, and all this
is nothing but a smoake; and he deales by the truth,
as men doe with an enemie in this case. First, they
labour to keepe him out from their confines, and if
they cannot doe that, then they levy forces to drive
him out from their land: So it is with a company
of

of carnall men; they would not looke upon the truth to be enformed by it. Well, Heare they must, and heare they shall, if they live under the power of the Gospel; but if they must heare it, they are contentious, and advise with this carnall friend, and that carnall Minister, and if they can get any man to plead for their lusts, that they may arme themselves against the blessed truth of God, they thinke themselves happy men.

If a Minister come home to the heart of a carnall wretch, that will buy, and sell upon the Lords Day, and say to him, Remember that thou keepe holy the Sabbath; then hee goes to some carnall man that buyes and sells as well as himselfe, and then he will have an army of forces against the truth of God. As the Apostle saith, *As Iannes and Iambres withstood Moses, so doe these men resist the truth, men of corrupt minds, and reprobates concerning the faith*; how is that? When *Moses* came to *Pharoah* to deliver the people of Israel, and when *Moses* shewed some signes and wonders; *Pharoah* would not yeeld to the Miracles, and therefore he called for *Iannes* and *Iambres*, and they made some appearances of Serpents, as *Moses* had done, and so *Pharaohs* heart was hardened: even so, When the Word of God is plaine, and the evidences of it are uncontrolable, then a carnall minde, sends for carnall quarrels, and pleas, and objections; and this hee doth to oppose the truth of Christ, and to make an army against the blessed Ordinances of God.

They

2 Tim.3.8.

They count it a matter of favour, if any man will deliver and refcue them from the truth.

As when this truth comes, You muft not buy
and fell upon the Sabbath, but you muft be holy,
as God is holy, &c. If this truth be troublefome,
oh they cannot beare it, and they would faine be
refcued, they count this truth an enemie to them,
and if any man will deliver them from the truth,
they thinke him a God; and they admire at his
judgement, and fay fuch a man is wife, and a deepe
Scholler, and he faith thus and thus, hee will defend
this as well as I: thus a man is fortified againft the
truth.

But an humble Soule will not doe thus. After
the VVord and Truth of God is revealed in this
kind, and all reafons anfwered: The underftanding
of this humble Soule, gives way and oppofeth not
the truth. Give an humble Soule Scripture for that
you fay, and hee hath done; and lets all carnall
counfells paffe: and all matters objected, and hee
faith, I am fully perfwaded of it, the truth is plaine,
God forbid; that I fhould quarrell with it. This is
for the underftanding.

Thirdly, If the truth be fo cleare and plaine, that   3.
hee cannot gaine-fay it, then hee turnes afide from
the authoritie of the truth, and will not fuffer it to
take place in his minde. This is the laft fhift which a
carnall man hath.

As, when a debtor is arrefted, at firft, hee
grapple with the Serjeant, but when hee feeth
the Bailiffe, or Serjeant, is too good for him,
                        V   he

hee labours to make an escape, and trusts to his feete, rather than to his hands. So it is with a carnall wretched heart. When hee cannot but confesse, and yeeld that the truth is plaine, and that hee cannot grapple with the truth, then hee falls flat against it: when his Serpent is eaten up by *Moses* Serpent; and all carnall pleas are eaten up by the truth, then hee is faine to withdraw himselfe from the authoritie of it.

From hence comes all those shifts: wee tell people they are miserable, and in a naturall, and damnable condition: Oh say they, God is mercifull: oh but (say wee) the mercy of God is such, that as hee pardons men, so hee purgeth them, and if mercy will save you, mercy will purge you too, and make you forsake your sinnes; doe you thinke that mercy will carry you, and your peevish proud lustfull hearts to heaven: No; hee will not; then say they, we will repent hereafter: and then we tell them againe, harden not your hearts, to day if you will heare his voyce, take mercy now while it is called to day?

God requires repentance now, and now you must humble your selves and repent. Yet the Soule goes on, and saith, wee blesse God, wee doe repent, and when wee sweare, wee cry God mercy, and though wee have beene, and are sometimes drunke, yet wee are sorry for it, then wee make them answer, and say, you say you are sorrowfull, but sound sorrow is ever accompanied with sound reformation. As the Apostle
saith,

saith, *Th.s same thing that you have beene sorrow-* | 2 Cor.7.11.
full, what carefulneffe hath it wrought in you, what
clearing of your felves, what indignation, and the
like ? And as the Wife man faith, *Hee that con-* Prov.28.13.
feffe.h and forfaketh his finne fhall finde mercy. Then
the finner replies, no man can doe thus. What,
would you have us without finne ? wee muft be
content to doe, as wee may. Thus you fee, they
yeeld to the truth, and cannot but confeffe that
it is plaine, but they take away the power of the
truth, and the command of it. You may fee
this in that curfed fhift of a carnall man. When
Balacke fent for *Balaam,* faying, *Come curfe this* Num.22.13.
people, and I will advance thee; The Lord met 19.
Balaam, and faid, thou fhalt not curfe them,
then *Balaam* rofe up early, and fayd to the Princes
of *Moab,* get yee home, for the Lord refufeth to
let mee goe with you : hee laid all the fault upon
God, as if hee had faid, I have a good affection
to goe with you, but the Lord will not give mee
leave. Well, when they came againe, hee faid,
tarry heere all night, that I may know what the
Lord will fay unto mee more. He would goe to ad-
vife with God, to doe that which God had formerly forbidden.

Thus the carnall heart goes to worke, when hee
cannot avoid the truth, and hee would faine have
fome refervations, and fuch exceptions, and hee
faith, is it not poffible that I may be drunke, and
adulterous, and covetous, and yet make a fhift to
goe to heaven too ? this is a wretched heart ; as *Ba-*

V 2 *laam*

laam did, so doe many, nay, the most of the world doe so ; consider the place of Scripture, and let me have your judgements in it ; *Hee that hath this hope* (saith the Apostle) *purgeth himselfe as Christ is pure.* He doth not say, he may and ought to doe it, but he doth purge himselfe ; and the Apostle *Peter* saith, *Be ye holy as Christ is holy in all manner of conversation.* Hee doth not say, hee may and should be so, but, be holy as Christ is holy, that is in truth and sinceritie ; as a child goes like his father, though not so fast as he. And as an Apprentice workes as fast as his Master though not so well ; and as the Apostle saith, *Abstaine from all filthinesse of the flesh and Spirit* : as if he had said, if there be ever a harlot or Alehouse in the world avoyd them, and all those appearances of evill, come not neare them. This is the condition that God requires. You heare all these truths, now let mee call for record from heaven, I would faine know what any wicked opposer can say against these truths ; oh that I could know your minds a little ! You that thinke a man neede not be so exact and precise, nay, you blame you children and servants for it. I know not what you would say ; except it be this : It is true, this is good, but doth any man do it ? and happy are they that can doe it, a man may be a man though not so good as another man, &c. away with those tricks, the Text saith, he that hath this hope purifies himselfe, as Christ is pure, though not for the measure yet in the same manner. Thou and I, and all of us

must

1 Iohn 3. 2.

1 Pet. 1. 15.

muſt doe it, or elſe we may caſt away all hope. The Lord be mercifull to us; if your judgements were humbled I can tell what you would doe, the heart that is humbled takes the truth, and yeelds to the authoritie of it, whereas a carnall heart Lords it over the truth; if it bee thus with thee, thy minde was never ſoundly enlightned, and as the Lord lives never humbled, never converted, and never brought home to the Lord; See what our Saviour ſaith, *why doe you alſo by your traditions tranſgreſſe the* Match. 15.3. *commandement of God.* They ſet their owne carnall traditions checke by joll with the commandements of God, they made the Command of God without any royaltie or power. They; were content to give Chriſt the hearing, but they turned aſide from the truth that ſhould have prevailed with them. If ever thou wouldeſt have the Word worke upon thee to doe thee good, then, whereas heretofore thou wouldeſt not come in, nor yeeld, now ſhew thy ſelfe to be humbled, and goe thy way home, and let this truth take place in thy heart, and be delivered into the forme of this doctrine now in hand, and when profaneneſſe, leud and ungodly ſports come : then remember this, and ſay, I muſt purge my ſelfe as Chriſt is pure, did Chriſt ever thus and thus ? did hee ever ſit up till twelve a clocke at night ryoting and banqueting? it is a truth, (oh Lord) let it take place in my heart, and let it be faſtened there. When the Lord hath a man in his ſetters, and breakes the heart with horror, *He openeth his eare to diſcipline, and commands* Iob 36.8,9,10. *him.*

V 3

him to returne from iniquitie. Hee doth not leave a man there and fay, this is the way and the truth, walke in it, but hee faith, I muft have that uncleane heart purged, and that carnall company abandoned, and fo forth; and fo the Lord faith to the Mini-fters, command that diffembler, and that hypo-crite, and that bafe wretch to come out from their ungodly practifes, and to yeeld to mee. Oh let the power and royaltie of this truth take place in your hearts, as it will doe, if you be Subjects of the truth. I charge you before God and his Angels if you know any command, obey it, and if you know any finnefull courfe, remember the commandement is plaine, you muft purge your felves as Chrift is pure. Let this word prevaile and have his authori-tie over you, and be not carnall hypocrites to op-pofe it now, and fo to be damned for it ever-laftingly.

2.
The will muft be fubject.
As the reafon muft be fubject to Gods Will, fo the will and affections muftbe humbled, and the frame that is contrary to this humility, is this; when the will and heart of a man (and that part whereby you fay, I will have this, and I will not have that) when this part doth not yeeld to the au-thoritie of Gods Word, when there is a kinde of Soveraigne Command in this waywardneffe of heart, and the heart would challenge a kinde of mo-narchiall authoritie, and would not be over-topped by the truth of God. This cannot ftand with any faving worke of humiliation. The generall is thus.

Ieremy,2.31. *As the people faid, wee are Lords, wee will come no more*
unto

unto thee, wee know what to doe. And as it is said in the Psalmist, *Our tongues are our owne, wee ought to speake,* Psal. 12.4. *Who is Lord over us?*

But some will say; How shall wee know, that *Objection.* our corrupt hearts, wills, and affections, doe thus over-power the truth of Christ? and challenge to themselves a soveraigne command? Here is the maine wound, and women that are weake in their reasons, are wonderfully refractory in their wils.

Wee shall know it by these three parti- *Answer.* culars.

First, the heart is weary of the command and wishes secretly there were no command of God to crosse him in his course, and to hinder him in his way of sinne. I will declare what I have heard wicked wrenches say in this kinde, because I will not teach men to be wicked. Hee wishes that there were no righteous God to bound him. The adulterer wisheth that there were no such Law as this, hee that burnes in his lusts here, shall burne in hell. And the drunkard wishes that there had never beene any Law made against that sinne, and hee saith, it is pitty that every man may not drinke what hee will: and the unjust person that would be stealing and pilfering, hee wishes that there were no Law against that sinne, and when the Word and his Consc'ence workes, and the Law makes havocke in his heart, and labours to throw him to the wall, Oh hee is weary of it.

Now a carnall heart thinks it is the greatest plague in

in the world, to be paled in within the compasse of Gods commands, that he may not doe what he list, but still, Word, and Conscience, and the Ministres checke him.

Malac. 1. 13.

When the Lord required, *Sacrifices at the peoples hands* in *Malachy*; They thought it a wearisomenesse, and snuffed at it. Wheat every morning Sacrifice? and every evening too? what a wearisomenesse is this? So, you ought to have morning, and evening prayer in your Families, how are your hearts affected towards it? doe not you say, what a wearisomnesse is this? why doe you tell us of prayer, and of humbling our Soules? This is a burthensome thing; this argues a heart that is above the truth, and that would be free from the truth, and justle it to the wall, therefore the wicked are

Rom 1. 28.

(as it were) in bonds and fetters, as the *Apostle* saith, *they did not like to have God in knowledge.* As if hee had said, it is a vexation to their Soule still to have conscience calling, be holy and humble, and be not proud, nor drunke, nor adulterous, their consciences flie in their faces, and the Word galls them, they doe not like to have this in knowledge. And therefore the Lord deales with them after their desires, and he gives them over to a reprobate mind, and to a heart that shall never imbrace the truth. You that have no delight to heare of your duties, and wish there were no Minister to controll you, the Lord will satisfie your desires, and gave you up to a reprobate sence. As if the Lord did say, you are weary of my wisedome, and goodnesse, neffe, and weary of my Word and Commands, I will eafe you of that burthen, you fhall have hearts that never fhall be moved with my Spirit; goe all you damned lufts and reigne in him, rule over him and make him a flave, and bring him downe to deftruction for ever.

If the Lord comes and will needs be revealed to him, then a fturdy heart layes violent hands upon the command, he difpofeth of it, and will not let the command difpofe of him; he hinders the pow-er of the truth that would draw him to God. As the Apoftle faith, *They withhold the truth in un-righteoufneffe.* The word in the Originall is, they imprifon the truth; as if the Apoftle had faid, you know you fhould not be loofe, nor covetous, nor drunke; is it fo confcience? are you drunke, loofe, and covetous ftill? when the confcience faith, I will be loofe and covetous ftill; and you will have the vengeance of God to follow you, and go to hell too. They doe imprifon the truth: The covetous man imprifons the truth, and hee muft have his co-vetoufneffe ftill; and the truth is imprifoned at the fuite of the adulterer, and he muft be uncleane ftill. And fo, the oppreffor muft lye, and diffemble, and oppreffe ftill, and therefore he juftles the truth and will of God to the wall. Hee takes the wall of Gods will. As the people faid, *there is no hope but wee will walke after our owne devices, and wee will doe every one the Imaginations of his evill heart.* They faid moft defperately, wee will doe it; heare it and feare, all you whofe confciences doe convince you of it; and you know that theeving and ftealing, and

2.

Rom.1.18.

Ier..18.12.

X   pettifhneffe,

pettishnesse, and peevishnesse, and all your profainnesse is forbidden; what saith your hearts to this? who disposeth of your wills in this case? doe not you say, wee will doe what wee list? As when *Samuel* had made an excellent Sermon, and told them the danger of having a King, *They said, nay, but wee will have a king over us.* So is it with many of you, Is this humilitie? The Lord saith, you shall not, and you say you will: oh fearefull! is this humilitie? aske but common reason; you say, wee must have, and wee will have it, wee have had our liberties and wee will have them, and so destruction too.

1 Sim.8.19.

3. Thirdly, This is the lowest and least kinde of rebellion; the Soule is content happily to doe what God requires, but it must be upon his owne conditions, and his owne termes. This is the last, and it argues no saving worke of preparation for Christ. The hypocrite is content that God shall have his glory, but hee must doe it. And a man is content to be painefull in his place, provided hee may have ease and honours, and parts, and preferments, and be respected, but when these faile, then God hath broken his condition, and hee will none. Thus God is at his dispose, and stands to his agreements. This is a cursed hypocrite. You can be content to heare, and pray that you may have some corruption, and that under the name of profession you may be adulterous and loose still. The God of mercy send some veine of good motions into your hearts, to awaken you if it be possible. Thus it is with some Ministers that are content to

be

be painfull in their places, so long as they may, have honour, and be respected; but if they misse of their end, they give over all. If there be any such here, you are hypocrites, and shall never be comforted upon these termes.

Now I come to the third passage of this triall namely, what it is that disposeth of our lives. A mans life aud conversation must be at Gods disposing. If the heart be distempered, and the reason be thus lifted up, then the actions of a mans life must needs be answerable: If those wheeles goe false, then the actions of a mans life must strike false. As they said, they would walke in their own wayes. And as the Lord faith, *I will bring their feares upon them, and my soule shall loath them because they did choose their owne devices.* That is, whatsoever their owne corrupt hearts would have, that they will take; and that way they will walke in. Not according to Gods will, but according to their owne rebellious hearts. So that all the practises of a mans course, are nothing else but as so many distempered behaviours of a rebellious carnall mind and heart. This disordered carriage discovers it selfe in three particulars.

First, when a mans life and conversation comes contrary to God, and goes a-breast against the Almightie: as they did, of whom the Apostle speakes, *Having their understandings darkened, have given themselves over to all lasciviousnesse.* They doe not what God will, but what their pride and idlenesse will. The Wise man saith, *Hee that is perverse in his wayes shall fall at once.* And the Apostle saith,

A mans life must be subject.

Esa. 66. 4.

1.

Eph. 4. 18.

Prov. 28. 18.

X 2 *When*

Rom. 6. 20.   *When you were the servants of sinne, you were free from righteousnesse.* What's that? Holinesse and Gods command had nothing to doe with them, that never tooke place in their hearts. Doe you thinke these mens hearts are at God disposing? See what the Apostle saith; *Fashion not your selves* Rom. 12. 2.   *like unto this world.* I onely appeale to mens consciences, what strange apparrell, and haire laid out, and what Spanish locks be there now adayes? who disposeth of these things? Oh forsooth, they are newly come up, and they must come up to thy head, and armes and all. These strange fashions doe argue strange distempers of spirit, and doe you thinke that God rules in those hearts and minds? and does God over-power those affection? when as they will not give him leave to meddle with a haire, or a locke, or an excrement: this is my judgement in this case. If it be so, that the Word of God may not take away a lap, and an excrement, our shame, and those things that are scandalous, then surely the Word of God must not plucke away our lusts. No, no, you are as far from subjection, as heaven is from hell, and as the devill is from the God of Hosts, The Lord speakes plainely by the Prophet *Zephany, He will* Zeph. 1. 8.   *visit all those that are cloathed with strange apparell.* When the fire shall flame about your eares, and the enemies come to plucke your feathers from your Caps, then you will remember this. You wou'd not have God to dispose of your cloathes, and haire, and the like, and therefore God will now dispose of your lives and liberties, and

when

when you lye upon your ſtraw, and ſee that you
muſt not goe gay to heaven, you would then be
content that the Lord ſhould diſpoſe of you, and
looke graciouſly towards you; and then you will
recommend your ſoules to God. But then the Lord
will make you anſwer and ſay, who had the deſpo-
ſing of you before, a drunken, adulterous, and faſhi-
onable ſoule, therefore let them ſuccour you now
get you to your faſhions, and let them make you
fry and roare in the faſhion; he that will not have
theſe baſe trifles to be at Gods command, ſurely
hee will never have his heart at Gods diſpoſing,
and therefore neither mind, nor heart, nor life.

Secondly, if God will over-rule wicked men a
little, and pull downe their trim faſhions, and will
gripe the Uſurer, and ſend the thiefe to remember
his Cheſts, and if the Lord ſay, you ſhall not be
rich, nor honourable, as you would: though you
ſeeke them never ſo faſt.

Yet ſecondly, they uſe all carnall ſhifts, and ſin-
full devices to come from that wofull condition
into which God hath caſt them. A man cannot
endure to be poore, and therefore hee will ſteale,
cooſen, or oppreſſe, and take any courſe to lift up
himſelfe.

Thirdly, Sometimes a man is content to be at
Gods diſpoſing in an outward conformitie, and
hee will doe the duties that God reveales, and leave
the ſinne that God forbids, and gives a charge a-
gainſt: but why will hee doe this? Hee doth not
theſe to honour God, but for ſome by and baſe
ends. As when the hypocrite prayeth, God doth

not:

2.

3.

not make him pray as the firſt moving cauſe of the worke, but his hypocriſie : and ſo the diſſembling profeſſor, that will profeſſe for advantage, to draw people to his houſe, or to ſell off his Wares more readily. And that people may ſay, Oh hee is a marvellous honeſt man; yes, and a covetous wretch too, and hee makes Religion as a ſtalking Horſe, for his luſts. You are not at Gods diſpoſing, unleſſe you be at his command in all theſe.

Thus you ſee the pride of a mans reaſon, in his will, his heart and life, wherein you ſee the deſperate villany of a mans nature ; and all is oppoſite againſt the God of heaven. If every bird had her feathers, and the worme her ſilke, and every creature their owne, what would become of the man that is proud. This is baſe enough, yet this is nothing to that Maſſe of haughtineſſe, and *Luciferian* wretchedneſſe that is in the heart. That a poore creature ſhould ſet his will againſt Gods will, and his way againſt the way of the Almightie; before whom the Angels ſtand amazed, and the devils doe tremble. God ſaith, I will have this, and the Soule ſaith, I will not have it : God ſaith, thou ſhalt not walke in this way, but the Soule ſaith, I will walke in it; God ſaith, thy reaſon, thy will, thy life, and all; ſhall be ſubject to mee; but the Soule ſaith, they ſhall not. Is not this infinite intollerable haughtineſſe? What, to make God no God, and that hee muſt have no will, no providence, and no rule over a mans life ? Oh! you that are guiltie in this caſe take notice of it. And, let mee

mee exhort you all that have heard the Word of God this day, and are poore ignorant men, and prophaine, and carnall hypocrites. Ignorance rules one man, and his corrupt lusts rules another man, but there is no good rule at all.

You have the Word of God and his counsels, and you have seene the way set out, now what remaines, but that you be intreated to goe home and humble your selves in secret, and say, this is my proud reason, my proud heart, and this is my proud carriage, it is I that would not submit to the command of Gods Word, And let every servant come in and say, this is my proud heart, my Master, and my Mistris may not speake, but I give word for word : this is my fault. And you wives reason thus : Now the Lord hath revealed the pride of my heart, and this is my proud reason and will, that would not yeeld to the command of my husband though never so warrantable. Let the child also humble himselfe, and say, when my father counsels mee, I turne my deafe eare ; and my mother is but a woman, and therefore I would have my owne will, and walke in my owne way ; this is my vaine minde. How many be there present heere this day, that are not willing to know some truths. You know you have made many conspiracies against the Word of God in the middle of the night, because your honours, case, and liberties lay at the stake, therefore the Word must not rule. If it be thus ; then to this day you are carnally minded, and stout hearted, and vaine. Goe home therefore I charge you,

and

and as you tender your owne good, goe into your private chambers, or elfe into fome fields, and there get downe on your kee, though your hearts will not bow, and fay, good Lord, I know, and confeffe it, to this day my carnall minde hath not beene brought under, and this vaine and idle converfation hath not beene ordered by thy Word : I have knowne much, and gone on in rebellion againft thee, and it is a wearineffe to mee to fanctifie the Sabbath, and hearing, praying, and other holy duties are a burthen to mee : to this day my heart is not prepared for mercy, good Lord, to this day I am a wretched carnall man.

This is fomething ; Now there is fome hope. And the Soule goes on further, and faith, Good Lord, what will become of my Soule, am I Gods to difpofe of? no, no, pride and peevifhneffe hath ruled mee, and I muft cloath my felfe as Pride would have mee. This is fomewhat indeed. And the adulterer faith, If the adultreffe come, I muft goe though I die for it. When the drunkard comes to pull you out, tell him of this, and fay, Who hath difpofed of you this day, and all your life, a drunken wretch, and a bafe queane. You have heard the Word of God checking of you, and yet nothing would doe ; Oh now at laft yeeld, and fay, The Lord hath not difpofed of mee. Now therefore labour that God may difpofe of you ; and let the mightie God pull downe that mightie heart : Challenge the Lord with his promife, and give him no reft till hee have mercy upon you. And you fervants, humble your felves, and fay, Wee

have

have beene proud and idle together, now let us
mourne and pray together. The time shall come
when you will be content that God should dispose
of you, and you shall desire the Lord to looke gra-
ciously towards you, and that God would take
away your corruptions, and that pride which ac-
cuseth you, and all those abominations that have
beene a shame and disgrace to you; therefore now
resolve with your selves, and say, Lord, take away
this sinne, and subdue that corruption, and doe
thou rule and reigne over my heart and life for
ever: let the power of thy truth carry mee, and
turne mee from my wickednesse, and over-power
this proud will of mine, and whatsoever vanitie is in
my life, good Lord take it away, and frame me after thy mind. When this time comes, say, That
a poore Minister did wish you good, and that you
had a faire offer. If you will be at Gods disposing,
in minde, in heart, and life, the Lord will prepare
a place for you in heaven, and ranke you there
amongst his blessed Saints and Angels for evermore.

If another mans servant come to demand of you
meate, drinke, and wages, you will say, You have
not beene at my command, therefore goe to the
Master that you have served, let him pay you your
wages: So it will be with you, if you goe to God
for mercy, and comfort, in that day, the Lord will
send you to your lusts, and new fashions, &c. but
if any man be Gods servant, then every thing shall
be fitted for him, and though that day be troublesome to the proud and haughtie spirit, yet it will

be

be a comfort to the godly, that they have submitted themselves to Gods Word. For, then Christ shall fill their mindes with wisedome, and their wills with holinesse, and their lives shall be made honourable and exceptable before him. Thinke of this, and labour to bring your hearts to it, that Gods will may be your will; and if you be humbled, you shall, and must be for ever comforted. Thus much of the triall of the truth of our humiliation.

The second part of the use.

Now I come to the second part of the use, that is, to examine the measure of our humiliation: for (as I conceive) all the difficultie of a mans course lyes here; and the cause why a man receives not the assurance of mercy from God that hee desires, or that comfort that hee might, it is all from hence (I say) becaufe he is not emptie. For if the heart be prepared, Christ comes immediatly into his temple, and the lesse wee have of our selves, the more we shall have of Christ. This is marvellous usefull, and therefore you must know that though the heart be truly humbled, and laid low in it selfe in truth, and the thing is done, yet there remaines a great deale of pride in the heart. Take a mightie Castle, though it be battered downe, yet there remaines many heapes of rubbish, and happily some of the pillars stand many Winters after: So it is with this frame of Spirit, in an high imagination, in these Towers of loftinesse. Though this *Dagon* of mans selfe be fallen downe, yet still the stumpes remaine, and will doe many yeares. And it will cost much horror of heart, and much trouble

ble

Cor.10.5.

ble before this haughtinesse of heart will be every
way pull'd downe, and made agreeable to the good
will of God. Though this distemper be marvellous secret, yet a man may take a measure and
scantling of it, and hee may know how much of How to trie
this cursed rubbish remaines in his heart, by these the measure of
foure particular rules. Humiliation.

First, looke what measure there is of carnall rea- The first par-
soning against the truth of God when it is made ticular Trial'
knowne, what measure there is of it, either subtilly
comming in upon the heart, or else that doth violently transport the Spirit against the Spirit, so
much neede thou hast of Humiliation, and so much
thou wantest of it. This is a cleare case. Every
Saint of God is willing to know the truths that
he shall doubt of, and is content to yeeld himselfe
to the truth that shall be revealed, and of which
hee shall be convinced; yet there remaines much
carnall reasoning against the truth. As the Apo-
stle saith, *Let no man deceive you ; intruding into* Coloss. 2. 18.
those things which hee hath not seene, vainely puft up
in his fleshly minde. The ground and root of this carnall reasoning, or the measure of it may appeare in
two causes.

First, There is a kind of perverse darkenesse in
the heart, still sticking in the minde and understanding, even of a gracious godly man. And
from hence, namely, out of this mistaking of the
minde, followes all that carnall reasoning: that,
howsoever the Soule is satisfied, yet it will not sit
downe, but still it sticks in this carnall reasoning,
and the sinner cannot conceive the truth, nor fa-

thom

thon the compaffe of it, by reafon of his owne
weakeneffe, therefore it is long before hee will be
perfwaded that it is truth, and that he is bound to
yeeld to it. When the wifedome of the truth is fo
plaine and evident, that hee cannot refift the cleare-
neffe of it, yet becaufe he cannot conceive of it, hee
thinkes, that he is not bound to yeeld thereunto.

Objection.

But fome will fay, fhould a man yeeld to that
which he cannot conceive?

Anfwer.

To this I anfwer. When the minde is fo farre
enlightened, that hee cannot gaine-fay any thing in
reafon, though he cannot compaffe the depth and
bottome of the truth, yet he fhould yeeld to it, and
rather goe with reafon, than follow his owne imagination, when there is no reafon for it. Juft fo it
was with *Nicodemus*. When Chrift fpake of the
worke of regeneration, hee faid, *Can a man be borne*

Iohn 3.9.

againe the fecond time? Well, Chrift opens the
myftery of regeneration, and the fecrefie of it the
fecond time, and when *Nicodemus* could not
comprehend what Chrift had fpoken, yet hee
would hold his owne, and faid, how can this be, I
cannot conceive it? becaufe hee could not comprehend it; therefore he throwes all away. Marke
how Chrift hits him in the right veine, and ftrikes
him to the bottome, and fee how hee tames him:
*Art thou a Mafter in Ifrael, and a Doctor in Law, and
yet art fuch a novice in this worke of regeneration,* downe
with that proud heart of thine. Lay downe all thy
carnall reafoning, and become a foole, and fo thou
mayft underftand this truth that is communicated
to thee.

This

This is ordinary amongſt us, for a man to ſay, I cannot beleeve it, I ſee it not, and I thinke not ſo; and yet they have no reaſon at all to carry them, but becauſe they cannot comprehend it by that light which they have, therefore they will not yeeld to any reaſon, becauſe they cannot ſee it by their owne light, they will not uſe Gods ſpectacles (as I may ſo ſay) looke how much of this carnall reaſoning thou haſt, ſo much pride thou haſt, and this is very much, ſpecially in the moſt ignoranteſt Soules.

Secondly, becauſe of the weakeneſſe, and feebleneſſe of their judgements, which are not able to hold a truth when they have it in their hands, but it goes away like lightening, and becauſe the minds of thoſe poore creatures, are over-worne with many thoughts, and curſed reaſonings, and troubled therewith, they grow unable to helpe themſelves againſt thoſe diſtempers. And hence it is, that though the Word of God be let in, and made cleare, yet a man ſtoopes to thoſe conceits, and curſed reaſonings that have beene attended to, ſo that they take off the power of the truth. As it is with a Ferryman; hee applies the Oare, and lookes home-ward to the Shore where hee would be, yet there comes a guſt of winde that carries him backe againe whether he will or no. So many a poore humble creature, that is truely wrought upon, and hath a true title to Chriſt; he applies his Oare, and would have aſſurance of mercy from Chriſt, yet the over-whelming of carnall reaſonings, and curſed ſuggeſtions (that are either caſt

Y 3   in

in or ſtirred up in his heart) throves him backe
againe, and takes off the power of the truth; inſomuch that he can ſee nothing, nor yeeld to any
thing for the good and comfort of his Soule. I
take this to be the ground of all the trouble that
befals a broken heart. Let any man under heaven
give me the reaſon of this; why any Soule that
is truely burthened for ſinnes as ſinnes, and hath
found God marvellous gracious to him this way,
why (I ſay) after all his cavils are removed,
and all his objections are fully anſwered, and all
controverſies are ended, and this often done ; yet
a poore broken hearted creature, will ſtill recoyle
to his former carnall reaſonings againe ; the reaſon is, becauſe all the anſwers that were given are
now forgotten, and all his cavils, and carnall conceits will be as freſh in his minde as ever they were,
partly from the haunt they have had in his minde,
and partly from that ſelfe-wylie waywardneſſe of
the heart, that is content to goe that way.

They that have beene long over-whelmed with
theſe curſed carnall cavellings, they will rather labour to oppoſe a direction, then to hold it, and to
walke in the comfort of it, onely becauſe of the
weakeneſſe of their underſtandings, and their carnall reaſonings are ſo violent againſt them. Vpon
this hinge it is, that (as I take it) all the objections
of a company of poore broken hearted ſinners doe
hange, and by this meanes they keep out that comfort which they might have ; and in the ſtrength
whereof they might walke all their dayes. I might
propound many inſtances, as thus; come to a contrite

trite Soule, and fay to him, why walkeft thou fo
uncomfortably, feeing thou haft now a title to mercy and falvation in Chrift? fee what he replies, I a
title to mercy? nay, I am utterly unworthy of that
title, it is a great gift and few have it, and I have
beene a vile wretch, and an enemy to God and his
glory; what, I a title to mercy? wee reply againe;
God gives grace to the unworthy, he juftifies the
ungodly, and not the godly, and if hee will give
you mercy too, what then? hee replies againe,
What mercy to mee? Nay, it is prepared for thofe
that are fitted for it; had I fuch a meafure of humiliation, and fo much grace; if I were fo and fo fitted; and if my heart were thus difpofed, then I
might have fome hope to receive it: wee reply a-
gaine. But have not you beene weary of your
corruptions, and are you not content that God
fhould doe that for you, which you cannot doe for
your felves; this is the quallification which God
accepts, and requires, and by which hee fits the
Soule for mercy; unleffe you have that other of
your own conceits you will have none, and fo you
deprive your felves of mercy; you have a childs
part, and a good portion too, if your proud hearts
would fuffer you to fee it. Then the Soule faith,
I would have the Lord fay to my Soule be of
good comfort, I am thy falvation; if the Lord
would witneffe this to mee by his Spirit, then I
could beleeve it: content then, onely let us agree
upon the manner how it muft be done, and how
God fhall fpeake it. Will you then yeeld it? Yes,
then know this, what the Word faith, the Spirit
faith,

faith, for the hand and the fword, the Word and
the Spirit goe both tog ther. For as the text faith,
My Word and my Spirit are one. Then take the
Word and lay thy heart levell to it, and fee it. The
Word faith, *Every one that is weary fhall be refrefhed*; Haft not thou beene weary, and haft not
thou feene fin worfe than hell it felfe? The Text,
the Word, the Lord, and his Spirit faith, Thou
fhouldeft come: and his Spirit faith, thou fhalt be
refrefhed. Oh faith the finner, I cannot finde this
affurance, and this witneffe of Gods Spirit, I cannot fee it, and I cannot beleeve it: Thus hee leaves
the judgement of the Word and Spirit, and cleaves
to the judgement of his finding, and feeling: and
thus he judgeth Gods favour in regard of his owne
imaginations, and not according to the witneffe of
the Word and Spirit: the Spirit faith, Thou art
fitted for mercy, but becaufe thy ignorant blind
minde conceives it not, hence it is, that thou fhut-
teft the doore againft the mercy of God revealed,
and that would be fetled upon thy Soule for thy
everlafting comfort. Thinke of this, and fay,
Whether is it fit that my wit fhould determine my
eftate, or the Word of God? Will you determine
the caufe, and perke into the place of judgement,
and fay, I feele it not, and I feare it not? Is not all this
carnall reafon? Here they runne amaine, even
a-breaft againft their owne comfort, and will not
receive the Word that might convey what comfort is needfull for them. I charge every poore
Soule to make confcience of refifting the word of
God, as you defire to make confcience of lying and
                                    ftealing:

stealing: this is a sinne though not so great as the other; make conscience of this carnall cavelling, pull downe those proud hearts, lay downe all those carnall reasonings, and let the Word of God rule you, and then comfort will come amaine. I take this for a truth; That, when the heart is truly humbled and prepared for mercy, and rightly informed and convicted of the way to salvation, the cause why the heart cannot receive comfort, it is meere pride of a mans spirit one way or other, it is not because hee will not, nor because God will not, but because hee listens to what his carnall reason saith, and not to the plaine Will and Word of God, I say, make conscience of it, and then comfort will come a maine into your Soules.

The second triall of the measure of our humiliation, is this. Looke to thy discouragements; For as the discouragements of thy course are, so is the pride of thy heart.

The second triall of the degree of humiliation.

If the streame run amaine here, there is much pride, if little discouragement, then there is little pride. This is nothing else, but when the Soule out of the feare of evill that it either feeles or expects, and the price that it puts upon it selfe, and that it lookes for from it selfe, it is nothing else but the sinking of the Soule below it selfe. As the Author to the *Hebrewes* saith, Consider him that endured such contradiction of sinners against himselfe, least you grow weary, and faint in your owne mindes. The word in the Originall is, as if their sinewes were shrunke. This is an undoubted argument and evidence of so much pride as this doth appeare. When

Heb. 12.3.

Z   a

a man is driven to a desperate stand, and comes to say a despondencie, and to lay himselfe too low, and is not able to beare the blow that God layes upon him : for, were the Soule as willing to take the want of good if God denie it, as to take good when God gives it, it would not be so discouraged. The heart is content to have good, but if God take away this good, he is not content to be at Gods disposing therein, but if this good goe away, hee sinks, and is discouraged, and this argues pride. The heart desires to have riches, and especially honors in the world, happily God denies this, and throwes filth and disgrace upon his person, and now the Soule is desperately downe and forlorne in himselfe : So much as thou hast of this, so much pride thou hast. Why art thou not content that God take away any thing ? the truth is, thou wouldest be at thine owne disposing, and that which thou wouldst have; thou art not able to want. Now because this is a thing that wee must take speciall notice of, know therefore that this discouragement appeares in these severall passages, and pride vents it selfe in them all.

First, This keepes a man from comming to the Word, when hee is called to it. Though the Word of God be never so plaine, and his calling to it never so cleare, yet he is loath to come at Gods call, and when he is come hee is quickly weary, and saith, what doe I heere ? Aske God that, because he thinkes, he shall not finde the successe that he desires, therefore he is loath to come to it, this is horrible pride. Thus it was with *Ionah* : he was
sent

1.
Signes of a
discouraged
heart.

sent to *Nineveh*, and because hee thought God would shew mercy to them, and hee should be accounted a false Prophet; therefore hee would not goe, but turnes to *Tarshish*, hee was not able to beare the crossing of himselfe.

Secondly, It damps the Soule, and (as I may so say) it knocks off the wheeles of a mans endeavours, when hee sets upon the worke, and it kills him at the roote : As the Prophet *David* saith, *why art thou cast downe within mee, oh, my soule? why* Psal.43.5. *art thou so disquieted within mee?* As a man that awakens from a swound, he wonders at himselfe : so did this Holy man. Thus it comes to passe, that the Soule recoyles upon it selfe. And the heart gives in, and hee (as it were) trips up his owne heeles; that, howsoever a man is able to doe duties, yet by reason of discouragements, hee is not able to put forth that which he can doe, for feare he should not doe that which he would.

Thirdly, this discouragement marvellously distempers a man after the worke. When the worke 3. is done by others if they finde exceptance, and have good successe, this comes like cold water upon the Soule, and then hee goes away and saith, Oh hee is fit for nothing and hee is unable to doe any thing; as if a man should say, Hee hath no light, because another mans candle burnes clearer than his : but after his owne worke, all his care is what will become of the businesse, and how his labour, and how his Sermon tooke, what approvement of his gifts, and what admiration of his parts, and if the acceptation of others answer not his de-

Z 2   sires,

fires, then his Soule finks downe, and hee is even
weary of himfelfe, his worke and all. If no man
commend him, and the worke is not approved,
then hee complaines of himfelfe this way and that
way, and begins to difparage himfelfe, onely to
fifh out commendation from others, and to fee
what they will fay, if they commend him, then he
goes away rejoycing, if not, then he finks; efpecial-
ly if he have not grace to go in fecret by prayer, to
quicken up himfelfe with fome promife after that
drunken fit. So the truth is plaine, it is wonderfull
to fee what pride there is. One man is ficke of the
fullen, becaufe the breath of man departs, and hee
falls fhort of that which hee expected. Though I
fhould prepare my felfe never fo well, yet if the
Lord did ftop my mouth now in the Pulpit, let me
be humbled, but comforted and contented therewith.

The third tri-
all of the mea-
fure of our
Humiliation. The third Triall of the meafure of our humiliation, is this difcontentedneffe in a mans occafions,
and fo much of this as there is, fo much pride
thou haft in thy heart, where this difcontentedneffe growes, there is this bitter roote of pride
alfo. The nature of a proud heart is not able to
beare any fuperiour, and if it be checked, it falls to
ftrange murmuring, and gaine-faying. This difcontentedneffe lets out it felfe in five particulars, and
there is a world of pride in them all.

Firft, the Soule will grudge at the difpenfation
of God, and fnarle at the providence of the Almightie, as if God had forgotten himfelfe. Hee
quarrels exceedingly with the Almightie, if God
anfwer

answer not his will, and his hearts defire. When
the Lord had prevailed with the peoples hearts,
and they had humbled themfelves, and the Lord
had turned from his wrath; fee how this man
falls out with God? Oh, faith hee, I thought fo Ionah 4.1.2.
much when I was in my owne countrey, that thou
wouldeft fave this people, and I fhould be accounted a falfe prophet, and thus my glory lyes in the
duft. You thinke God is beholden to you for
your prayers, and faftings, and you fay, how is it
that after all our prayers, yet wee have not comfort, fuch a man is cheered, and fuch a poore creature is refrefhed, and yet they have not the parts
that wee have, and they have not prayed as wee
have done, thou haft fhewed mercy to them, and
therefore why not to us too. This is horrible
pride.

See how a proud Soule juftles God out of the
place of his providence, and brings the Almightie
to his barre, and to his judgement; and the heart
begins to reafon inwardly, and fometimes vents it
outwardly, and faith, had the Lord given mee that
grace, and fitted a place for mee, I could have done
much for God, and fome good to his Church, and
I could have miniftred much comfort to others:
this is the Englifh of it. As if hee had faid, had the
Lord beene fo wife (to devife a meanes to effect
his glory) as I am, then great matters might have
beene done. This is to make a mans wifdome a-
bove God, and his mercy, grace, wifedome, and all.
Oh! this is devillifh pride.

Secondly, It flights all mercies received, and
all

Z 3

all that God beſtowes from day to day; becauſe
hee cannot have what he would, therefore hee cares
not for it, and he regards not what hee hath. As
Hamam ſaid, *All this honour and theſe riches availe me*
nothing, ſo long as I ſee the Iew Mordecai ſitting in
the gate. This one thing denied him, made him
not to regard whatſoever hee had; and it was not
onely ſo with *Haman*, but even with good *Ionah*;
When God had prepared a goard, becauſe he tooke
it away againe ſuddenly. *Ionah* tooke on exceedingly, and forgetting all Gods mercies in the
depth he quarrels with heaven, and when the Lord
ſaid, *Doſt thou well to be angry? yes* (ſaith hee) *even*
to the death, thus he commends himſelfe. The reaſon is, the ſoule is like a ſullen child, who, becauſe
his coate is not garded as he would have it, therefore hee is diſcontented and will have none at all.
Therefore the Soule ſaith, as they did of the two
little fiſhes, here are five barly loaves and two
fiſhes, but what are theſe amongſt ſo many people:
So the Soule ſaith, oh! he hath nothing, and he can
doe nothing, and God frownes upon him, &c. but,
hath not God given you a care and conſcience to
reforme your lives? and hath not he done this and
that for you? Oh yes, but what's this to that I
might have had and that I would have? oh, downe
with that proud heart.

3.   Thirdly, The diſcontented Soule will quarrell
with his owne condition whatſoever it is, though
hee had a condition of waxe as the Proverbe is, he
is never pleaſed nor quieted, but hee hath ſtrange
Imaginations in his minde, and ſtrange liftings up
                                                    of

Hoſter 5. 13.

Ionah. 4 9.

Iphn 6. 9.

of his owne conceits, and hee faith, If God had set me in such a place answerable to my gifts and parts then such a thing might have beene done: but God hath put him (as it were) under a clod, and therefore hee hath no care of himselfe as God hath had no care of him: nay, let him have that condition which hee desires, and he falls out with that too; *Rebecca could not be contented without chil-* Gen. 25. 22. *dren, and yet when shee had conceived, and the children began to strive in her wombe,* she faith, *if it be so, why am I thus?* So it is with a proud discontented heart. Hee must have this, and hee wil have that, and if there be any weaknesse, hee sinks downe in his sorrow.

It is a strange passage of good *Iosuah* (when the Iosh. 7. 7. Lord had discomfited the hoast of *Israel* by the men of *Ai,* see how he complaines, saying, *Alas, (oh Lord God) wherefore hast thou at all brought this people over* Iordan, *to deliver us into the hands of the Amorites, would God wee had beene content to dwell on the other said* Iordan As if hee had not begged Gods blessing, and had not seene Gods hand in succouring of him before, and yet now because he had not what he would, hee takes all in the worst sence. And as *Moses* said, when the Lord had called him to goe before *Pharoah, send by whom thou should'st send.* As if God must not dispose of him, Exod. 4. 13 because hee had not that eloquence which hee desired.

Fourthly, as he quarrells with his condition, so 4. hee becomes weary of his life, and will needs die in a pet, because God answers not, and his humour
is

is not fitted, therefore hee will away from the
world, no man fhall fee him any more, neither
will, hee fee any man. Thus it was with good *Eliah,*
when hee faid, *Lord take away my life, for I am no bet-*
ter than my Fathers. So it was with *Ionah,* and with
Iob. You *women thinke of this.* It may be your huf-
bands will not fpeake to you, as you would have
them, and then you wifh ; Oh, that you had dyed
in fuch a fickeneffe,&c. Downe with thofe proud
hearts. The Lord hath given you life, and continues it, that you may feeke to God, and yet you
will needs die in a fullen fit : it is mercy that you
may live to feeke mercy.

Fifthly, in conclufion, when the Soule hath
thus quarrelled with God, and flighted all mercies, and quarrelled with his condition, and is
grown weary of his life and all, then the Soule comes
to a defperate diftraction in himfelfe, and a wonderfull thought feazeth upon the Soule of a difcontended man, that his heart is almoft driven beyond himfelfe, and out of this comes a great deale
of madneffe in the wicked ; and it doth much hurt
to the good too. His thoughts runne in a marvellous hurry one upon another, and makes the Soule
unfit to doe any good to others ; or to receive any
good from others. Here is the caufe : when God
hath opened your eyes, and the wrath of God
firft began to purfue you , then you could have
beene content to fall into a river, and to make away
your felves : Now, what if God will have you
beare his hand, and will not give you grace yet ;
why doe you quarrell againft God ? Oh fit downe
and

2 King. 19 4.

Iob 3, 10, 11,

and humble your selves with meekeneſſe and calmeneſſe, add wonder that you are not in hell; what if you had beene damned long age? Thus it was with *Rachel*, ſhee would not be comforted becauſe her children were not; So it is with thy Soule, thou muſt have what thou wilt, or elſe thou wilt not be comforted. Now, there are two objections againſt the former truth, which I muſt remove and anſwer before I goe any further.

The diſcouraged ſinner begins to juſtifie him- *1. Object.* ſelfe in his courſe, in the apprehenſion of his owne inſufficiencie, and he ſaith, I ſee by daily experience that I am not fit for the place where God hath ſet mee, and it goes off marvellous heavily, the Lord takes away the hand of his providence in ſtrenthe-ning me, and the hand of mercy in comforting mee: what would you have a man to doe? is it fit for a man to beare up himſelfe, in a kinde of ſenſe-leſneſſe of the hand of the Almightie? or is it not rather fit to ſee the hand of God in his diſpleaſure? and to ſit downe and licke the duſt, and to be ſo farre from venturing upon the worke, as to let it alone? This is the plea of a diſcouraged ſinner, and therefore hee thinkes hee doth well, to ſit downe *Rachel* like, and not to be comforted, but to let his Soule fall in ſorrow.

I confeſſe, it is true. The heart truely humbled *Anſwer.* ought to be, nay, it cannot be brought to ſee it ſelfe in every kinde, ſo that it judgeth it ſelfe un-worthy of the leaſt mercy, and worthy of the hea-vieſt judgements, it cannot be but contented in abaſement; But yet there is a great difference betweene a heart truely humbled, and a difcouraged heart. And the difference appeares in two things.

The Soule thinkes it doth marvellous well to be thus difcouraged, and that there is no other Humiliation but this. Know therefore this double difference.

First, This Humiliation leaves the Soule more calme and better able to undergoe a light blow when it hath borne this. Whereas after difcouragement the Soule is more full of trouble, and more unable to beare any trouble, becaufe it hath funke under this: If the Lord denies to the humble Soule that which hee would have, it makes him more able to beare the want of any thing: but the difcouraged Soule flies off, and is leffe able to beare the hand of God in the want of any thing. Humiliation feafons the veffell, and makes it more wide, and more fit to hold liquor, but, difcouragement cracks the veffell, and makes that it will hold nothing at all. And Humiliation is like the Tentures that ftretcheth the cloath, and makes it more fmooth and plaine: humiliation ftretcheth the Soule, and makes it more humble and meeke : but difcouragement rends the heart, and makes it more unfit to undergoe that which is laid upon it. As Saint *Paul* to the *Hebrewes* faith, you have forgotten the exhortation which faith, *My fonne, defpife not thou the correction of the Lord, nor faint when thou art rebuked of him.* The word faint, that is, difcouragement is fpoken of by our Saviour, when hee was moved with compaffion towards

the

The differences betweene a heart humbled, and a heart difcouraged.

Heb. 12. 5.

the people becaufe they fainted, and were as Matth.9.36.
fheepe fcattered abroad having no Shepheard. So
I fay, doe not fufferthy felfe to be fo farre fcattered with thefe troubles, that thy heart be unable
to gather up himfelfe againe. As it is with fome
ftubborne child, when his father comes to correct him, he fnuffes, and falls into a fwoune with
griefe, whereas another child is quiet and takes
the blow quietly, and goes away contentedly
without any manner of fainting. So the heart
truely humbled, is like the child that takes the
blow quietly; but the difcouraged Soule faints,
and is not able to beare the hand of God in this
kind.

Secondly, the fecond difference is this. As The fecond difference.
Humiliation ever leaves the Soule calme and qui-
et, after the hand of God had beene upon it: fo it
makes the Soule more ready, and puts a kind of
abilitie and cheerefulneffe in attending upon God
in any fervice, without any hankering after his
owne ends, and without this quarrelling, and this
drawing backe from the Lord. So, that becaufe
hee hath borne the hand of God, therefore it is
much more ready that the Lord fhould difpofe of
duties, and the fucceffe of them, feeing it hath
found God going out with him heretofore; and
he faith, the truth is, fometimes the Lord did deny me that mercy which I defired, and bleffed be
God for it, for by this meanes I found my proud
heart humbled and brought downe; therefore if
God will have mee doe any duty, I will doe it,
and if hee caft fhame and difgrace upon me in it, I

am

am contented. This is a heart truly humbled : but, the difcouraged Soule not receiving that ftrength and affiftance in his duties that he would have, hee is marvellous untoward, and unwilling to come to the like fervice any more. For feare hee want fucceffe, and fhall not be able to beare the want of it. Humiliation (as it were) levils the heart, that the Lord Iefus may take place there ; but this difcouragement deludes the heart, and makes it more unfit for Chrift. *Iohn Baptift* was fent to prepare the way for Chrift, that every Valley might be fill'd, and every Mountaine and hill brought low. The high way wherein Chrift went is the heart, and the ditch or valley, was the defperate difcouraged heart ; aud this fainting of heart unfits the way for Chrift, as well as the mountaines and hels. As Humiliation levils the heart, and makes it fit for Chrift, fo this difcouragement dulls and unfits the Soule to be quickned, and to give way to a Saviour, and to entertaine him. Humiliation takes off the knottineffe of the heart, and makes it runne fafter in the way of Gods Commandements, but difcouragement hangs a backe byas upon the Soule, that, as a backe byas holds a boule, that a man cannot make it run right to the marke : fo this difcouragement is like the backe byas, and thats the reafon why a difcouraged heart comes fo weakely to holy duties, as to conference, fafting, and the like. If a man goe to fafting, and prayer privately, if God give him not that fucceffe that he would, and hee cannot doe it as he defires ; oh, how hardly is he drawne to it againe :

but

Luke 3.4.

but the humbled Soule faith, bleffed be God, though I had not that ftrength, and that fucceffe that I defired, yet if the Lord fhall call mee to the like duties, I will goe againe though I cannot doe as I would. So then, know that there is no ground for difcouragement; thats a finne: be contented, yet for ever humbled.

If the next place, the difcontented perfon thinkes 2. *Obiect.* his way reafonable, and it is warrantable for him now and then to be difcontented, and therefore he faith, what would you have a man doe? you know it, and I finde it, that God hath denied mee many abilities in thofe duties, which hee calls for at my hands; others have gifts, and power, and abilities; but I am weake and feeble, and can any man, nay, fhould any man be contented with this; would you have a man content with his fin? I cannot beleeve it; thus, becaufe they fee fuch deadneffe and untowardneffe of heart, therefore they conceive that they doe well to be difcontended, and they caft all the fault upon their finne.

This is a defperate hinderance to all good du- *Anfwer.* ties, and therefore I anfwer it thus. It is true, the Lord allowes it, and warrants it that thou fhouldeft be difpleafed with thy finne, not to be under the power and rule of it, and the humble heart is at the difpofe of God, and at the difpofe of finne, but yet be wife in this cafe. It is one thing for a man to be difcontented with his corruption, and it is another thing to be difcontented with that condition wherein he is.

Thou mayft (and oughteft to be) difcontented
with

with thy pride and corruption; and with thy unbeleefe, but, take heede that thou be not difcontented with the weakeneſſe of thy gifts and parts. This
is damnable pride; and it is an argument that thou
art not content to be at Gods finding, and this is
thy diſeaſe twenty to one.

Now, that thou mayeſt know whether thy diſcontentment is for thy corruption, or for thy e-
ſtate and the weakeneſſe of thy parts; I ſhew it thus:
hee that is diſcontented with his ſin, will never ſin
in his diſcontentedneſſe. As we uſe to ſay of im-
moderate ſorrow. If any man looſe a friend and
begin to grieve and ſorrow exceſſively, wee uſe
to ſay, take heed that you mourne not out of meaſure. Marke what hee replies; may not a man ſorrow for his ſinne? To this I anſwer. Art thou ſorrowfull for ſinne, and wilt thou ſinne deepely in
thy ſorrow, and reſiſt the good will of the Lord?
no, thou haſt loſt a friend, and meanes, and therefore thou mourneſt.

This is carnall ſorrow, and in this thou never
ſorroweſt for ſinne, he that is ſorrowfull for his
ſinne, will not ſinne in his ſorrow; it is for thy condition that thou art ſo ſorrowfull, and diſcontented. Is it not ſo with thy Soule? that thy heart is
toſſed up and downe in a reſtleſſe diſquiet, and art
thou not out of the command of thy ſelfe? and art
thou not hurried up and downe in a confuſed lum-
ber in thy minde, becauſe thou art not fit for duties? if it be ſo with thee, then thou doſt ſinne
deſperately in thy diſcontentment.

It is a rule in warre; If any Army be once ſcatte-
red

red and difperfed, it will hardly come on againe, becaufe it is put out of ranke and order. So that Soule is difcontented with his eftate, that is made unfit for duties, and unweldy in them; that difcontentment which unfits a man to be at Gods difpofing, it is not the worke of humiliation, but a worke of pride. But it is fo with thee, thy difcontentment makes thee unable to beare Gods hand, and the want of any thing; and makes thee more unfit for duties; and it is not finne, but for thy weakeneffe in gifts, and for thy condition, and therefore thou art poffeffed with this pride of heart.

The fourth and laft note, and triall of the meafure of our humiliation is this. If thou wilt know how much pride is in thy heart; then confider how thy Soule ftands in regard of the word and truth of God that croffeth thy beloved lufts, and thofe corruption to which thy Soule hath cleaved in the time of thy wretchedneffe; and in this there are two paffages.

The fourth and laft note of the meafure of our humiliation.

First, fee how thy heart behaves it felfe, in regard of the ftrict commands of God.

Secondly, in regard of the keeneft reproofes, and the fharpeft admonitions that are fuggefted into thy heart. See how thy heart is able to beare the reproofe of an enemy, or the admonition of a faithfull Minifter of God, when hee meets with thy darling luft. When thy heart comes under thefe commands, and thefe reproofs, if thou find thy heart fwelling, and bubbling againft the truth, and thy heart begins to be angry with the Word, and Minifter, and all; then know this, that

certainely

certainely so much of this as there is in thy heart,
so much thy soule wants of Humiliation. Is not
this pride that the Soule should lift up it selfe a-
gainst the Lord of heaven? and take the way of
Gods Word? and when the frothy franticke heart
of a man will beare downe the command of God,
and let the command of God fall to the ground,
rather than let a corruption fall; is not this infinite
pride?

You must take notice of this distemper in severall passages. When the Prophet came to that
wicked King *Amaziah*, and said to him, *Why hast
thou sought after the Gods of the Heathen, which
could not deliver their owne people out of thine hand?*
then the King said to him, *Art thou made of
the Kings counsell? forbeare, why shouldest thou be
smitten?* Then the Prophet said, *I know that God
hath determined to destroy thee, because thou hast
done this, and hast not hearkened to my counsell.* A-
maziah was naught, and God did deale with him
accordingly: So, when Gods Word doth meete
with mens hearts, and lusts, they are mad; and if it
were not for shame, and feare; they would pull a
man from the Pulpit.

2 Cron. 25.
15,16.

Objection.   But some may say, can the Saints of God be
thus transported with this vile distemper?

Answer.   Yes, this colericke distemper of heart, sometimes creepes in upon a good Soule, but the
difference will appeare afterward. *Aza* was a
strange man; though Divines hold him a good
man: When *Hanani* the Prophet dealt plainely
with him, and said, *Thou hast done foolishly in resting*

1 Chron. 16.
7,10,11,12.

ing upon the *King of Aram, &c.* See how the King entertaines this; *Hee was wrath with the Seer, and put him in prison:* But see what befell the King. He never saw good day afterward: hee fell into many finnes; fo the Lord leaves a man to his corruptions; *and after that hee fell into a strange difeafe in his feete:* A ftrange thing that God fhould leave a good man in this mifery; thus hee dyed; and all this was for oppofing the Word of God. This is the nature of a peevifh collericke fpirit. The humble fpirit doth not quarrell with the Word of God, *but receives it with meekneffe,* Iam.1.11. *and with a quiet ftill fpirit.* If any finne bee revealed, and if any dutie be commanded, hee beares the Word without contending; unleffe it be now and then, for flefh will have his bouts. Looke home therefore into your owne hearts, and families: how can you beare the checks and reproofes of a Mafter or Miftris, when they fay, you are idle. And fo, you wives, when your husbands reprove you; is not all on in a light flame? Oh, this is infinite and intolerable pride. You may be good fervants and good women; but it is ftrange if you be fo.

But you will fay, how fhall a man fee a diffe- *Objection.* rence in all thefe?

I fay, the Saints of God, and the finners; the *Anfwer.* faithfull and the faithleffe; all have this in their manner and meafure; but this corruption is poyfon in the heart of a good man. Its true, the Saints of God are fometimes difcontented and difcouraged, but when they fee it, they are content

that the Word should worke upon them againſt
it, and they complaine of theſe wretched hearts,
and when they find this diſcontentedneſſe, they
quarrell with themſelves for it; and a good man
would even pull out that heart which quarrels a-
gainſt the Word of God, and hee ſaith, is not this
the Word of God by which we muſt be ſaved?
and is not this the power of Chriſt? and ſhall I
be angry with it? God forbid: But, theſe diſtempers are naturall in a carnall man, and though hee
be reproved for a fooliſh faſhion; yet hee will
hold his corruptions ſtill; hee puls, and the Miniſter puls; the Miniſter would pull downe his
proud heart, and take away his corruptions; but
hee will have his pride, and fooliſh faſhions, and
his corruptions ſtill: then keepe them, and periſh
with them, and know that thou art a wretched
man: the humble heart contends with his corruptions and ſinnefull diſtempers, and hee is not
quiet therewith. As it is with a Treaſon; If it be
revealed to a Traytor, and a good Subject: the
Traitor keepes it ſecret, but the true Subject reveales it, and complaines of the Traytor, and the
Treaſon; and calls for juſtice againſt them: ſo
it is with a gracious good heart. Hee ſeeth theſe
curſed diſtempers, and ſometimes findes bublings
of heart againſt the Word of God, and this
ſhakes his Free-hold; yet when a good heart ſee-
eth the Treaſon, hee doth not joyne with it, but
hee complaines to the Lord of it, and ſaith, Oh
Treaſon Lord; this vile heart will be my deſtruction; good Lord, reveale it yet more to mee, and

take

take away all thefe corruptions; take thou the poffeffion of me, that I may ferve thee here, and be with
thee for ever hereafter. Thus much for the ufe of
Examination.

Is it fo, that the heart truely humbled, and pre- *Ufe 3.*
pared for mercy is content to be at Gods difpofing, as you have heard? then what fhall we fay
of thofe that lift up themfelves againft the Almightie: this difcovers the fearefull condition of
every fuch Soule. It is certaine the haughtie Soule
is furtheft of all from Salvation; how prove you
that? he that is furtheft off from Humiliation, he
is fortheft off from the beginning of grace here,
and from perfection afterward: the gate of grace
is meerely here; for, except you become as little
children, that is, except you be humbled, you
cannot enter into the Kingdome of Heaven; a
proud heart is farre from grace now, and from
happineffe in the end of his dayes. For the difco-
very of this mans mifery, let mee lay open foure
Particulars: and I would have my felfe and you to
confider them, that our proud hearts may be pull'd
downe.

First, Pride is profeffely againft God, and is the Foure degrees
moft directly contrary to the whole being of God, of a proud
and that in the whole man. mans mifery.

Indeede all finnes are nothing elfe, but a kinde Pride oppofes
of croffeneffe to the Lord of Hofts, and a kinde God.
of thwarting of fome Attribute or other in God:
As, falfhood croffeth the Truth of God, impatience croffeth the patience of God; and in-
juftice, croffeth the Iuftice of God: So that, thefe

Bb 2 finnes

finnes goe againſt the Almightie in their meaſure,
ſome againſt one Attribute, ſome againſt another:
but a proud heart ſmites at the whole Eſſence
and Being of God: Nay, hee doth as much as in
him lyeth, labour to take God out of the world,
and he would be God himſelfe, and have no God
but himſelfe: The Lord doth principally Attribute two things to himſelfe, which can be in
none but himſelfe. God is the firſt of all cauſes,
and the laſt End of all. All things were created
by him for himſelfe; hee made all by his Will,
and Wiſedome; and by his Wiſedome, and Providence, he governes all for himſelfe. Before any
thing was, God was, and all muſt returne tribute
of praiſe and thankſgiving to God. A man may
be like God in mercy and in Juſtice, though
not ſo perfectly, yet ſincerely; and a man may be
like God in other of his glorious Attributes, but
God onely is firſt and laſt. If it be a creature,
then it was made: but here is the venome of a
proud heart, hee would be firſt and laſt. He doth
all by His owne power, and hee will promote his
owne praiſe in all that he doth. As the great King

Dan.4.3. *Nebuchadnezzer* ſaith, *Is not this great Babel that
I have built, by the might of my power:* I built it;
there is the firſt, *for the honour of my Majeſtie,*
there was the laſt. So, it is not the wiſedome, and
pleaſure of God that muſt ſtand; but his owne
proud heart: it muſt not be what God commands,
but what hee would have; all of a proud man is a-
gainſt the Almighty.

   The Saints of God have wondred that the
                                             Lord

Lord is able to beare a proud man that thus out-
braves God in regard of his speciall prerogatives;
it is a wonder that God sends not some lightning
from heaven and even stampe them to powder, and
send them downe packing to hell suddenly, I take
this to be the sinne of the devills that are now
chained up in eternall darkenesse, untill the judgement of the great day, nay, I take this pride of a
mans Spirit, of his minde, his reason, his will
and affections, to be another old man of sinne.
Drunkennesse is a limbe of this old man, and so
is adultery and other sins, but pride is (as it were)
the old man it selfe.

This is the brooder, the Spawne, and the very
mother from whence the sinne against the Holy
Ghost growes, and there wants nothing but the
illumination of the truth to come in upon the
heart: when a mans understanding is enlightned
and this Illumination comes upon the heart, and he
is violently carried against the truth with indignation, this is the sin against the holy Ghost.

Secondly, as Pride is opposite to God himselfe, **2.**
so it is opposite to the covenant of grace, beleeve Pride opposeth
and live; for the truth is, that which wee call infi- the covenant
delitie and the ingredients of it, are pride; as the of grace.
Apostle saith. *Where is boasting then? it is excluded,* Rom. 3 7 °.
by what Law? by the Law of workes? no, *but by the*
Law of faith. If there be beleeving, then away with
carnall reasoning and with pride.

Therefore I may say by collection, if faith ex-
clude all boasting, than pride or boasting opposeth the covenant of faith. Faith is excluded by
this

this pride of a mans spirit; and by the swelling of heart: and the holy Prophet *Habakkuk* saith, *The Soule that is lifted up in himselfe, is not upright within him*; hee that swells and bubbles up in his heart, and puffes up himselfe against the Word of God, he hath no upright spirit within him, but the just man shall live by his faith; above all, see that place in *Esay, Harken to mee all you stout hearted ones of the world which are farre from righteousnesse.* Let mee speake to all you stout-hearted men and women that are here this day; you that swell against the truth of Christ, and will not come under the power of Gods Ordinances, you are farre from righteousnesse. The further you are gone in this sin, the further you are from the righteousnesse of God. A stout hearted man is a thousand miles from righteousnesse.

Habak. 2, 4.

Esay 26. 12.

Drunkards and adulterers are farre enough from it, but a proud man is (as it were) twenty hundred thousand mile from it; he is farre from the covenant of faith.

Faith goes out for all that it hath to another, it reacheth up to heaven for all; it wants meate and nourishment, and therefore it goes to Christ for all; and pride onely rests upon it selfe for all; faith gives the glory of all that it hath to another; but pride takes all the glory to its selfe. Faith goes to another for strength in what hee doth, but pride rests upon it selfe for strength: So that, though all sinnes hinder the worke of Faith, yet, pride hinders it more than any thing. You that thinke it a brave matter to be proud; and you must not

not buckle to the Minister, and you must doe what you list, you are stout-hearted men; but you are farre from beleeving men. The more faith, the lesse pride; and the more pride, the lesse faith.

Thirdly, As pride opposeth God himselfe, and as it opposeth the covenant of grace, so it followes from the two former, that the proud Soule upon these conditions (that it is in) shall never receive any grace from the Lord. Set your hearts at rest for that. You may swell, and lift up your selves, but if ever you receive the worke of grace, and mercy upon these termes; I will be your bond-man for ever. For, he that is professely contrary to the grace of God, that gives all; and hee that is contrary to the covenant of grace by which all is conveyed; let him set his heart at rest, for ever receiving any mercy. The Lord himselfe is not able to endure the sight of a haughtie spirit; hee cannot looke upon him, much lesse will he live with him. Hee beholds the proud man a farre off, hee drives a proud man farre from heaven. The Lord deales by a proud man, as a man doth that is carried with indignation against his enemie, he will not looke upon him: So it is with the Lord, hee will not be within the ken of a proud man, and if the Lord doe come neere a proud man, wo to him that hee doth so. The Lord resists the proud. Hee whets all the sharpest arrowes of his vengeance, and shoots them all against a proud man. You broken hearts consider this. The Lord gives grace to the humble, but the proud man must be content with his portion, he shall be resisted, not received;

3.
A proud soule is farre from mercy.

Psal. 138.6.

he

hee fhall be refifted, not converted ; nor faved, nor
fanctified. Hee may bid farewell to all grace, hee
fhall never have it upon thofe termes : and as God
intends no good to him; fo a proud man comes not
within the fcope of mercy, nor of that redemption which Iefus Chrift hath wrought and purchafed. Chrift came not to c. ll the righteous, that is,
them that looke loftily in regard of what they doe.
You ftout hearted people, thinke of it. The Lord
Chrift came not to call you. The devill calls, and
you may goe to him : but Chrift came to call and
fave the poore broken hearted finners. It is faid
of Chrift, *That hee was annointed of the Lord,* to
preach the glad tidings of the Gofpel, to whom ?
to the meeke, &c. You meekened Soules fhall heare
good newes from heaven. But there is not any
one fillable of one promife in all the Gofpel, that
any proud fpirit can conceive to belong unto him.
If I could feparate all the good from the bad, I
would have the good to ftand by, and heare thefe
good newes that I have for them ; and if you proud
hearts will come in and yeeld, they may be yours
too. You that tremble at Gods Word, and are
willing to doe what God fhall command ; if there
be any fuch here this day, as I doubt not but there
are many, then know, that the Sonne of man
came to feeke and fave you ; it is good tidings.
Nay, in the Lord Iefus Chrift are all the Treafures of wifdome, and knowledge, and out of
this fulneffe of holineffe, and happineffe, he fils all
your meeke hearts, and he will give all grace according to your neceffities ; here is newes of falvation,

Efa.61.1.2,3.

vation, life, and comfort from heaven. But to whom is it? Chrift came to feeke and fave them that are loft: that is, them that are loft in their owne apprehenfion; but the proud man was never loft in himfelfe. A loft man in the Wilderneffe is content to be guided into his right way: but the proud man faith, hee will be filthy and fafhionable ftill, therefore hee was never loft, and Chrift never came to feeke nor fave him.

All the meanes of grace that God gives, will never benefit a proud man. So that now, it is as poffible, nay, more poffible for heaven and earth to meet together, than for a proud man to come to heaven, except God give him a heart to ftoope. No man can receive benefit by the Word, except he be under the power of it; if the waxe be not under the Seale, how can it receive any impreffion? As the Apoftle faith, *They were delivered into the forme of that doctrine propounded.* The forme of the Gofpel tooke place in their hearts. There is no Soule can get any benefit by the Gofpel, but hee muft receive what it reveales, and what it commands, hee muft doe; and what it forbids, hee muft labour to avoyd; but a proud heart is above all meanes, and therefore the Word will not, nay, it cannot worke favingly on him. As thofe wicked ones faid, *Our tongues are our owne we ought to fpeake, who is Lord over us?* What reproofe fhall awe me, faith a proud heart, I will be led by my owne lufts? Your owne reafon leades you, and your owne wills rules you; your owne minds, and your lufts; and what your hearts will have, they muft have.

All meanes doe a proud man no good.

Rom.6.17

Pfal.12.4.

You

You stout-hearted ones that are resolved not to yeeld, nor to come under the grace of God: you will not have your affections framed, nor made more teachable; then, seeing you will not be taught, be for ever deluded; goe your way, and be for ever hardned; and for ever cast off from the presence of God, and goe downe to the bottomlesse pit; you will have your owne wills, therefore goe to your owne places, for that is all you can have. You that are the faithfull of God, and know any such, mourne for them.

4.
A proud mans end is exceeding fearefull.

Fourthly, againe, the destruction of a proud man is both certaine, exceeding heavie, and it is like to be marvellous fearefull. There is nothing to be expected and hoped for, but totall ruine, and that suddenly, and unconceiveably to every proud spirit that beares up it selfe against the blessed God of heaven. Let mee open it thus. A proud man is marked out for Gods Iudgements, and is made (as it were) the white against whom all the arrowes of his vengeance are fully bent. When *Amaziah* would needs out-bid the Prophet in his advice, and said, forbeare, *why shouldest thou be smitten?* I will forbeare (saith the Prophet) but know what shall befall thee, *I know the Lord hath purposed to destroy thee, because thou wilt not harken to my counsell.* You that are acquainted with your stout-hearted husbands, and wives and friends, and know how your children bandy themselves against the blessed truth of Christ; goe in secret and bemoane their estate, and pray for them, that if it be possible, destruction may be prevented:

2 Chron. 25. 15, 16.

goe

goe in secret and say, it is my husband, or my wife, or my child, that yeelds not to the direction of the Word, and therefore howsoever wee may live a while together, yet I know God hath decreed to destroy him, and her. Thinke of this with your selves you that are proud, and say, If I will not be exhorted, then I shall be destroyed; I cannot avoyd it. Oh, me thinks if every proud spirit, would write this upon the palmes of his hands, and upon the tester of his bed, that he might see it wheresoever hee goes; how would his heart sinke within him. When thou goest abroad, say, for ought I know I shall never returne home, God hath decreed to destroy me. And when thou lyest downe think thus, for ought I know I shall never rise more. It is not the word of man, but of the Almightie. When the Lord would (as it were) frame a path for destruction, hee sends a proud heart. If once the Lord intend to destroy a People or Nation, hee gives them over to pride of heart. *The sonnes of Eli did not harken to the voyce of their* 1 Sam. 2. 1 *father, because the Lord meant to destroy them*: hee gave them over to proud hearts. Nay, the proud Soule is not onely the ayme of Gods wrath, but as the Lord determines destruction for him; so, hee brings destruction first upon him. When the Citizens said, *wee will not have this man to rule over us*, then the King was wroth, and said, *bring hither those mine enemies, and slay them before mee, &c.* Luk. 19 4. 2. There was no delay, nor no mitigation of the punishment to be granted. Oh thinke of this, all you proud spirits. Indeede the Lord will con-

found

found all the wicked in the Day of Judgement, but he will execute even the fierceft of his Vials of his vengeance againft a proud man; and when the Lord fhall fay, where are thofe wretches mine enemies? then the Minifters of God fhall come in and fay, this man was a drunkard; and this man an adulterer; Yes (faith the Lord) I will plague them anon, but, where are thofe mine enemies? thofe ftout-hearted men or women, that hated to be reformed? let me fee thofe damned and deftroyed for ever. And for ought I know, God hath a ftrange indignation in ftore for them. Nay, it fhall be fo executed upon a proud man, that there fhall be no reclaiming of it, and God will not be perfwaded to pitty him. *They fhall call upon*

Prov.1.26,27, *mee* (faith the Text) *but I will not anfwer, they*
·8.   *fhall feeke mee early, but they fhall not finde mee.* So that, it is no wonder though a company of rebellious wretches have no comfort upon their deathbeds, and though a thoufand devils feaze upon them, and hurry them downe to hell, it is no wonder, I fay; cry and call they may, but God will not heare them : Nay, the Lord will laugh at their deftruction, and mocke when their feare commeth; It is a griefe for a man to be in mifery, but to be laughed at, that is a plague of plagues. But, to have mercy rejoyce in the deftruction of a man, this makes the plague out of meafure miferable.

If any man fay this is a falfe doctrine, and this is too fharpe and too keene. Brethren, wee dare doe no other, and wee can doe no leffe, and you had better heare of it now while you may prevent it,
then

then to heare of it, and feele it hereafter when there is no remedy. But, here is the maine wound of our Miniftery, you will not ftoope nor yeeld to our Miniftery. We fpeake not in wrath and anger, (as you imagine) but in mercy ; wee now preach againft a proud heart, that you may be humbled, and finde mercy, and fo be comforted and faved for ever. Therefore take your owne fhame, and the Lord prevaile upon thofe hearts ; which word and counfell cannot worke upon. And the Lord now fit you for mercy, that you may receive mercie from the Lord. That is all the hurt wee wifh you. Oh, that you would fo heare of thefe plagues that you might never feele them. The Lord hath an old grudge againft a proud heart. Go away you proud hearts, feare and tremble. When you are gone from the Congregation, doe not fay, What if he fay fo, we fare well enough yet, and we fee none of all thefe judgements, and all this winde fhakes no corne : no, no, once ftoope and come in, and take the yoake of Chrift, and the Lord make it eafie. Goe in fecret and reafon thus, good Lord, have not I onely lifted up my felfe againft man, like my felfe ; but againft God, and againft his Ordinances ? and hath God yet fhewed me mercy in fparing of mee ? and it is yet mercy that I may bow my body, though I cannot bow my proud heart : oh what mercy is this ! You wives, thanke God that yet hee hath fpared your husbands, and that yet they have breath and being here : pray to God, that they may lay about them for humble hearts, that fo they may finde mercy againft the evill day.

Our

Our God is very mercifull, but it is no contending with him. Did ever any man provoke the Lord
and prosper? Come in therefore, shame your selves,
that the Lord may humble you now, and shew
mercy to you hereafter.

Vse.4.   The last Vse is for Exhortation: You see the
woe and misery of a proud spirit. What remaines
then, onely this; be exhorted, as you desire to
finde favour with God, and to receive mercy
from him, now be content to be at his disposing.
Walke in this way, and ayme at this marke; strive
hard for it, and put forth the best of your abilities, that you may get humble hearts. You must
not thinke that every lazie wish, and every desire
will serve the turne; and that it will be enough to
say, is it so that a proud heart is so farre from
heaven? I would I had an humble heart, and so
forth. You must not thinke that God will bring
you to heaven before you be aware of it, and that
a humble heart will droppe into your mouthes.
The Saints of God have alwayes had it before
they received Christ, and thou must have it too,
if ever thou wilt have him, therefore make it a
chiefe part of thy daily taske to get it; *And suffer
not thine eyes to sleepe, nor thine eye lids to slumber,
nor the temples of thy head to take any rest,* before
thou hast this gracious disposition of spirit. You
see the price, the worth and excellency of this
blessed grace, doe not now let this grace lye lay,
cast it not into a bye corner; but in all your desires covet this, and in all your hunting up and
downe

downe after commodities, prize this more than all, and labour to get it above all.

I know one man hath his eye upon the world, and another on his pleasures, and every man saith, what shall wee eate, and drinke, and wherewith shall we be cloathed? but doe not thou say, how shall I be rich, or honourable, but how shall I get this humble heart? What is that to thy Soule, that thou art rich and a reprobate; and that thou art honourable and damned. If thou be once humbled; then thou art past the worst. It is the choisest good, and the chiefe of thy desires should be for an humble heart. Now to draw our hearts to this, there are three considerations that may be seasonable, and serviceable to this end. And they are these.

First, Consider, that it is possible to have an humble heart.

Secondly, Consider the danger if you have it not, I will not give a rush for all that you can doe without it, though you live *Methuselahs* dayes.

Thirdly, Consider the exceeding benefit that will come by this grace.

For the first, It is possible for any Soule present (for ought I know or that he knowes) to get an humble heart. This may be a provocation to us, to set upon this dutie. If a man had no hope to get this desire, hee would have no heart to use any meanes for it. A man had as good sit still, as rise up and fall, as the Proverbe is. But, seeing it is possible, why may not thou, and I, or any man here get an humble heart? and therefore seeke to the Lord

1. Motive.

Lord for it, and say, there hath beene many as proud hearts, and as stout as mine (though I have beene like a devill for my pride) yet they have had this grace, and therefore (Lord) why may not I have it as well as they? who knows but God may give me an humble heart too? though my heart be now stout, and stubborne, and rebellious, yet Lord, I see no command that forbids mee not to expect this mercy, and I see no truth that excludes mee; no, the Lord saith in his command, humble your selves under the mightie hand of God. Yea, the Lord hath appointing meanes for the working of this grace, and hath ever blessed those meanes for the good of others, and why not me Lord? Lord, hast thou blessed these meanes to others? and made them stoope and yeeld, why wilt thou not blesse them to mee too Lord? who knowes but God will doe it for me, as well as he hath done it for others?

Therefore goe thou to God, and say, The truth is (Lord) I confesse this haughtie and this rebellious heart of mine will not come downe, it is not in mans power to pull downe my proud heart: No, it is not in the power of Angels to humble a proud heart: Lord, now take this stout heart, and humble it, and doe what thou wilt with it; didst thou not tame the heart of *Manasses*, that Witch and Blood-sucker that made the streets of *Ierusalem* to swim with blood? Didst not thou humble him? and didst not thou bring downe the proud heart of that sturdy Iaylor? and didst not thou tame the heart of proud persecuting *Saul*? Didst not

no thou make him come creeping in upon his
knees? Lord, thus thou haft done; Lord, humble
me too. Thus importune the God of heaven. Nay,
preffe God with his promife, and with that en-
gagement whereby hee hath tyed himfelfe. *The* Efa. 2. 12.
*day of the Lord of Hofts fhall be upon every one that
is lifted up, and that is proud and lofty,* (faith the text)
*and he fhall be brought low, and upon all the Cedars of
Lebanon that are high and lifted up, and upon all the
Oakes of Bafhan.* That is, upon all mighty, vile,
fturdy, and unreafonable men; and what then?
they fhall be brought full low, and the Lord alone
fhall be exalted in that day. The day of the Lord
fhall be upon all flefh; preffe God with this promife, and intreate the Lord to remember it, and
fay, Lord make all thofe fturdy hearts yeeld. Oh
that this may be the day, and that I may bee the
man, and that my heart may be the heart, that thy
mercy and grace may onely bee admired and wondred at. Thus you fee, that God may doe as much
for you, as he hath doe for others; and it is poffible to get an humble heart, therefore labour
for it.

Secondly, as it is poffible to get an humble heart, 2. Motive.
fo, confider, that if you miftake your felves, and
faile here, the danger is wonderfull defperate, and
fearefull; and therefore ufe fo much more care and
diligence, not to be deceived therein. If you miffe
here, never looke to bee faved nor recovered hereafter. Miffe now, and you are undone for ever, its
as much as your foules be worth: as your Humiliation is, fo your Faith, fo your Sanctification,
and

and your obedience will bee. If that be nought, all will be nought. It is obferved by Philofophers, and Phyfitians, that if there be any fault in the firft difgefture, it cannot be amended in the next, if the ftomacke digeft the meate ill, the Liver can never make good blood : So a wound here, can never be amended. If the bottome and foundation of a building, be not found and fubftantiall, though the frame be never fo neate and handfome, yet there is no mending of it, it muft be all puld down, and the ground-worke made more fure; and therefore when men fet up fome maine pillars to uphold a houfe, they digge deepe and low, and fet them ftrong : So, if this worke of humiliation be not deepe and low enough, all the frames of a mans profeffion will fall downe, there is no mending of it. If the foundation of the houfe be found, though the thatch and fpars flye off, there is fome helpe : but if that be nought, the houfe will downe whatfoever the other be : So, many weakeneffes may be fuccoured, and the heart may be fuftained under them all, if this worke of humiliation bee good; but if a man once proove falfe here, thy faith and obedience will be nought, and the Spirit of God will never dwell in thee, nor quicken thee.

Matth.7.13. See what our bleffed Saviour faith, *Strive to enter in at the ftraite gate, &c.* This gate, or this entrance into life, is Humiliation of heart. When the Soule is loofened from, and bids farewell to finne, and himfelfe, then the gate is opened. And as it is in other wayes; If there be but one way or gate into an houfe, and the traveller miffeth that gate, hee

loferh

loſeth all his labour, and muſt go back againe: but
if he once get in at the gate, he is ſafe enough then.
So it is here. There is a moſt narrow way of Gods
Commandements, and there is but one way or
gate into this happineſſe, it is narrow, and a little
gate; and a man muſt be nothing in his owne eyes,
and if you miſſe this gate, you loſe all your labour, and ſhall never come to Salvation. If a man
could heare and pray all his dayes, yet, if his heart
be not humbled, he, and his profeſſion ſhall goe to
hell together. In Saint *Matthew* the concluſion is
very peremptory; when the Diſciples were contending who ſhould be higheſt; Chriſt ſet a childe
in the middeſt of them, and ſayd, *Except you become* Math. 18. 3.
*as little children, you cannot enter into the Kingdome
of heaven.* You may doe any thing with Infants,
and all that they have to doe, is to cry. Unleſſe you
have humble hearts, you cannot enter into heaven.
He doth not ſay, You cannot be great men, or, you
cannot goe farre into heaven; but he ſaith, *You cannot enter.* So then, the danger being ſo great, and
the miſtaking ſo full of hazard, and ſeeing it is poſſible to have it, therefore let us uſe all diligence to
make this worke ſure.

Thirdly, conſider the marvellous good that 3. Motive.
God hath promiſed, and which hee will beſtow
upon all that are truely humbled. And let all theſe
bee as ſo many cords to draw us to looke for this
bleſſed frame of heart. We have need of all the
motives in the world. I know it is a hard matter
for a man to lay downe himſelfe, and his parts and
all his priviledges in the duſt; I ſay, it is marvel-

lous irkefome and tedious to the nature of a carnall man; but, it will quit all his coft in the end. When we fhall tafte of thofe fweete benefits that come by an humble heart, and have gotten Jefus Chrift; and mercy from him: then it will never repent us that we have fpent fo many teares, and made fo many prayers, and ufed fo many meanes to pull downe the pride of our hearts; Oh brethren, thinke of it, See and confider the admirable benefits, and the exceeding great good that will come to you thereby. The good things that come by a heart that is truely humbled, they are fpecially foure, and with thofe the truth and fubftance of whatfoever the heart can crave and defire.

The firft benefit of an humble heart, is this, by this meanes we come to be made capable of all thofe riches of the treafure of wifedome, and grace, and mercy that are in Chrift: and not onely of the bleffings for a better life, but of all things in this life fo farre as they are good for us.

First, wee are made capable of all thofe treafures of wifedome, grace, and mercy that are in Chrift, and for this caufe was Chrift fent to preach glad tidings to the meeke as you heard before. All the Gofpell, and all the glad tydings of it doe belong to an humble Soule. And the Prophet *Malachy* faith, *Behold, I will fend my meſſenger to prepare the way before me, and the Lord whom you ſeeke ſhall ſuddenly come into his Temple. Iohn Baptiſt* was Chrifts harbenger, and hee made way for Chrift, and when the way was prepared, Chrift came immediatly: *we are the Temples of the holy Ghoſt* (faith the

Malac. 3. 1.

the Apoſtle.) Now, if the heart bee once prepared and humbled, looke then immediately for
Chriſt. Are you not content to have Chriſt dwell
in your hearts? If you will be humbled, and ſo
prepared; there is neither want of love, nor ſpeed
on his part. This ſhould marvellouſly lift up the
heart of every man, to ſeeke for this bleſſed grace.
If thou are truly humbled, care not for the love
of men; the love of Chriſt will ſatisfie thee. And
though thy father, and mother caſt thee out of
doores, and thy husband tumble thee out of his
bed, yet if thou be truely humbled, Chriſt will bee
in ſtead of father, and husband, and all comforts
to thee. God hath but two thrones, and the humble
heart is one: So the Text ſaith, *I dwell in the high* Eſa. 57. 15.
and holy place, with him alſo that is of a contrite and
humble ſpirit, &c. If the Lord Jeſus come to dwell
in thy heart (and that he will doe) if thou be truly
humbled) then certainely he will provide for thee
all needefull comforts for this life. See what *Ze-*
phanie ſaith, *Seeke yee the Lord all yee meeke of the* Zeph. 2. 3.
earth, which have wrought his judgement, ſeeke righ-
teouſneſſe, ſeeke meekeneſſe, it may be you ſhall be hid in
the day of the Lords anger. When all things threatned deſolation and deſtruction; ſee who they
were that had ſafety promiſed, onely the meeke.

But ſome will ſay is it not better for a man to Object.
be proud with the proud, and to play the Beare
amongſt Beares, and the Lyon amongſt Lyons, and
to ſhift for one?

No (ſaith the text) *ſeeke meekeneſſe.* The humble Anſwer.
Soule may take this to himſelfe as his part and
portion:

portion: If there should be desolation amongst us
as there is in *Bohemia*, in the *Palatinate*, and in
other Counteries, the humble soule shall be hid.
When the mightie tall trees are blowne down by
strong winds, the little shrubs may be shaken a little, but they stand still; they are safe and sure,
when the mighty Oakes are either horribly shaken, or puld up by the rootes: So, if ever you will
seeke safety and deliverance, seeke meekenesse, and
then you shall be hidden. When the proud heart
shall be weltering in his blood, the Lord will provide a shadow to succour, and comfort you. If
Christ dwell in your hearts, he is bound to all re-
parations.

1. Benefit.

    Secondly, as Humiliation of heart doth estate a
man into Christ, and his merits, and all provision
in this kinde; so, it gives him the comfort of all
that good which hee hath in Christ. There are
many that have a right to Christ, and are deare to
God, and yet they want much sweete refreshing
that they might have, and as the Proverbe is, They
never see their owne, becuase they want this Humiliation of heart in some measure. To be truely
humbled is the next way to be truely comforted.

Esay. 62, 8.

The Lord will looke to him that hath an humble con-
trite heart, and trembles at his word, that is, an humble Soule, a poore Soule, a very beggar at the gate
of mercy; the Lord will not onely know him (for
he knowes the wicked too in a generall manner)
but he will give him such a gracious looke, as
shall make his heart dance in his brest; thou
poore humbled Soule, the Lord will give thee a
glympse

glympfe of his favour when thou art tryed in thy trouble, and when thou lookeft up to heaven, the Lord will looke downe upon thee, and will refrefh thee with mercy. It is that which God hath prepared as a fweete morfell for his child, hee will revive the humble. Though the proud man fhall fit and fwelter himfelfe in his trouble, yet the Lord will not onely be in the houfe, and heart of an humble man, but looke to him and revive him. It is the condition to which the Lord hath promifed confolation, and this humiliation of heart is the maine terme of agreement, upon which God hath ever fhewed mercy. *Behold, I ftand at the doore and knocke, if any man heare my voyce and open, I will come in to him, and fup with him, and hee with me.* As when men fup together and eate in the fame difh, it argues a fweete rejoycing in the familiaritie one of another. I know you would faine have much comfort; the Lord now knockes, if you will but open the doore, he will come into your hearts, and he will bring his owne provifion with him; even the fweete cordialls of his grace and comfort; and he will refrefh you with thofe confolations which the eye of man hath not feene, and the eare of man hath not heard,&c. onely the Saints of God fhall feele them. *Every valley fhall be filled,* (faith the text) *and every hill fhall be brought low, and the crooked things fhall bee made ftraight, and then all flefh fhall fee the falvation of the Lord.* When fhall they fee it? when thofe things are done that are there promifed. *Iohn Baptift* was to make way for Chrift,

Efa. 57. 15.

Rev. 3. 26.

Luk 3. 5, 6.

Chriſt, and the text ſaith, *Every valley ſhall be filled,*
that is, every deſperate diſcouraged heart, and
every mountaine ſhall be levelled, that is, every
proud heart ſhall be humbled; and then all fleſh
ſhall ſee the Salvation of God; here is the cauſe
why we finde not the aſſurance of Gods love that
we might and ought to have; there are mighty
mountaines of carnall reaſonings, and ſtrange miſts
of diſcontentment betweene Chriſt and the Soule;
and theſe keepe off the light of Gods love in Chriſt,
which elſe would ſhine in our faces for our everlaſting comfort. Now bee humbled and throw
away all thoſe diſtempers, and then the Lord Jeſus who comes with healing under his wings will
comfort you, and you ſhall ſee the Salvation of
God. There is a Chriſt and Comfort in him, if
your Soules be humbled, you ſhall ſee it, and finde
the evidence of it. When the Sunne is neere ſet-
ting, becauſe there is a mountaine betweene us and
it, therefore we thinke it is ſet when it is not;
whereas if a man were on the top of it, hee ſhould
ſee the Sunne cleare : So it is with all thoſe mountaines of carnall reaſonings, they ſtand betweene
the Lord Jeſus and thy Soule, and that is the reaſon
why thou ſeeſt not the light of Gods countenance
ſhining upon thee.

The third be-
nefit of an
humble heart.
Mat. 23. 12.

Thirdly, we alſo may have glory in this comfort that we have in Chriſt; as our Saviour ſaith,
whoſoever exalteth himſelfe ſhall be abaſed, but whoſo-
ever humbleth himſelfe ſhall be exalted. Hee doth not
ſay, If ſuch a man and ſuch a woman humble them-
                                          ſelves,

felves, but the words are univerfally to bee under-
ftood; whatfoever thou art, bee thou humble, and
the Lord fhall lift thee up. It is impoffible that the
exaltation and a glory of an humble Soule fhould
be hindred by men, or devils. Let the devill and all
his inftruments labour to caft fhame and difgrace upon thee; nay, bee thy condition never fo
bafe and meane in the worlds account, be thou
humbled, and it cannot bee hindred, but that the
Lord will exalt thee; the Lord hath promifed it,
and thou being as thou fhouldeft be, the Lord will
doe what he hath engaged himfelfe to. The Lord
many times for want of this, leave men of great
parts, and gifts; in the lirch: they fret and are grieved exceedingly, becaufe fuch a poore man findes
acceptance, and is approoved of, and yet no man
lookes after them; If you know any fuch, tell them
it is by reafon of their pride, they feeke their owne
honour, and not Gods; they are not humbled but
feeke to exalt themfelves, and God will abafe them.
Let them fawne and flatter, let them flatter and diffemble never fo much (as moft men doe toget honours) yet God will abafe them. And for this caufe
God blafts one mans endeavours; and withers another mans gifts, and brings him to fhame, becaufe
he is proud; whereas the humble foule that is content to honour God in his abafement, the Lord will
fet up that man in mercy and goodneffe; the Lord Pfal. 25 9.
will teach the humble in his way. Doth the Lord
care for any mans parts or gifts, or for his honor and
refpect? No, the Lord hath chofen things that are 1 Cor. 1. 28.

not

not, that is, things that in the eyes of the world are
accounted as nothing, those hath God chosen, to
confound the haughtinesse of the hearts of proud
men in this kind. See how *David* answered *Michall* when she mocked him, and sayd, *Oh how glorious was the King of Israel this day, &c.* Is not this
a goodly matter for the King to doe? See how he
answers her, it was before the Lord who chose mee
rather than thy father and all his house, and commanded me to be ruler over his people, and therefore I will play before the Lord, and if this be to
be vile, I will yet be more vile. Thy father was
naught, and thou art so too, and he is gone to his
place. The meanest in all the place will honour the
humble heart, but though happily the people
may feare a proud man, yet they will never honour
him in their hearts.

Fourthly and lastly, we have blessednesse in all
that appertaines to an humble heart. *Whosoever
humbles himselfe as a little childe, shall be greatest in
the Kingdome of heaven;* He doth not say, hee that
is greatest and most loftie may haply be great, but
he that is humble, and trembles at every truth of
God, and every truth prevailes with him, and every terror awes him, hee shall be greatest in the
Kingdome of heaven. You take it as a disgrace to
be reprooved by a servant, or an inferiour; but the
humble soule takes it whatsoever it is, and is willing to be reprooved by any; and hee that doth
thus, shall be in the highest degree of grace here,
and shall bee greatest in the glory of heaven, and
be

2.Sam.6. 20, 21.

The fourth
benefit.
Mat.18.4.

be lifted up to the highest pinacle of glory, the wider and deeper a veſſell is, the more liquor it holds; So, Humiliation makes the heart wide and deepe : and as thy humiliation is, ſo ſhall bee thy Faith, and thy Sanctification, and Obedience is anſwerable, and thy Glory ſhall be ſuteable. Now to conclude all.

Doe you conſider that it is poſſible to have an humble heart? doe you conſider the danger if you have it not? and doe you conſider the good that comes by an humble heart, and doe you ſit ſtill? as he ſayd in another caſe. Me thinkes your hearts begin to ſtirre, and ſay, hath the Lord engaged himſelfe to this? Oh then (Lord) make mee humble. Me thinkes your countenances ſay ſo; The Lord make mee and thee, and all of us humble, that we may have this mercy. Let mee make but this one queſtion to your Conſciences, and give me an anſwere ſecretly in your ſoules; when the Lord ſhall cloſe up your eyes here, and put an end to your pilgrimage; would you not be content to dwell with Chriſt in heaven? which the Apoſtle did account his greateſt happineſſe, to bee ever with the Lord; wee ſhall be ever with Chriſt to comfort us, when we ſhall be no more with ſinne, to vexe and trouble us: would not you be content to be with Chriſt? mee thinkes your hearts ſay, that's the end and upſhot of all, that's the end why we live, and pray, and heare, that we may be ever with him. And doe not you meete with many troubles, while you are members of the Church Mi-

The concluſion.

litant?

litant? I know you have sometimes diſtempers
without, and troubles without, would you not
have comfort againſt them all? and what would
you give that Chriſt would looke in, and aske
how your Soules, doe, and ſay thou art my redee-
med, and I am thy Redeemer. No, you know, all
fleſh deſires it. Would you not bee content to
have ſome honour in the Church? and to leave a
good name behind you, that the diſgraces which
wicked men caſt upon you, may not bée as a blot
upon your names? and when you ſhall bee no
more, and you ſhall bid adue to friends, and honours, and meanes, would you not be bleſſed? and
though you would bee content to be the meaneſt
in the Kingdome of heaven, what would you give
to be the meaneſt in heaven? let mee put a condition to you; get but humble hearts and you have
all. Men, brethren, and fathers; if there bee any
Soule here, that is content in truth and ſinceritie
to be humbled, and to be at Gods diſpoſing in all
duties to be done, doe not you make too much haſt
to goe to heaven, the Lord Jeſus Chriſt will come
downe from heaven and dwell in your hearts, hee
will ſit, and lye, and walke with you; his grace
ſhall refreſh you, and his Wiſedome ſhall direct
you, and his Glory ſhall advance you; and as for
happineſſe, take no thought for that. Everlaſting
happineſſe, and bleſſedneſſe, lookes and waites for
every humble Soule; Come (ſaith happineſſe)
thou that haſt beene vile and baſe, and meane in
thine owne eyes, and in the contempt of the world,
                                                    come

come, and be greateſt in the Kingdome of heaven.
Brethren, though I cannot prevaile with your
hearts, yet let happineſſe, that kneeles downe, and
prayes you to take mercy, let that (I ſay) prevaile
with you. And anſwere me now, who would not
be humbled? If any man be ſo regardleſſe of his
owne good : I have ſomething to ſay to him, that
may make his heart ſhake within him. But, who
would not have the Lord Jeſus to dwell with
him? who would not have the Lord Chriſt by the
glory of his grace to honour, and refreſh them?
and that he ſhould ſet a crowne of happineſſe upon their heads? Mee thinkes your hearts ſhould
earne for it, and ſay, oh Lord breake my heart, and
humble me, that mercy may be my portion for
ever. Nay, me thinkes every man ſhould ſay, as
Saint *Paul* did, I would to God that not onely I,
but all my children, and ſervants, were not onely
thus as I am, but alſo (if it were Gods will) much
more humbled, that they might be much more comforted and refreſhed.

The Lord in his mercy grant it. Let all parents
labour to have their children humbled, and every
maſter his ſervant. This will give them cheering
of heart in that great Day of accounts : when
paleneſſe comes upon your face, and leanneſſe to
your cheekes, then I know you would leave your
children a good portion; then get their Soules
truely humbled. Me thinkes it cheeres my heart to
conſider of it; if a man could get his owne heart, and
the hearts of all, truely humbled; when hee leaves

the world, if hee could but say, my wife is humbled, and such a child, and such a child, is humble; how comfortably might he goe away, and say,
though I goe away, and leave wife, and children behind me, poore and meane in the world, yet I leave
Chriſt with them. Brethren, though you care not
for your ſelves, yet care for your little ones, never
leave exhorting of them, never leave praying for
them, and for your ſelves too, that you, and they
may get theſe humble hearts. When you are gone
this will be better for them than all the beaten gold,
or all the honours in the world.

There are many that have heretofore ſtood out
againſt the Lord, and they would not come in, nor
yeeld to the conditions of mercy; all thoſe proud,
haughty, and rebellious ſpirits that have ſtood out
againſt Gods Truth, his Word, and Miniſters,
and have ſtood out long; ſome twentie, ſome thir-
tie, and ſome fortie yeares, let all ſuch feare and
tremble; and now reſolve not to ſtand it out any
more; but ſince the Lord offers ſo kindly to comfort you, and to honour you upon your Humiliation; Now kiſſe the Sonne, be humble, yeeld to
all Gods commands, take home all truthes, and be
at Gods diſpoſing. There muſt be ſubjection, or
elſe confuſion: will you out-brave the Almighty
to his face, and will you dare damnation? as you
love your ſelves take heed of it. As proud as you
have beene cruſhed and humbled. Where are all
thoſe *Nimrods*, and *Pharaohs*, and all thoſe mighty
Monarchs of the World? The Lord hath throwne
them

them flat upon their backes, and they are in hell this day. Therefore be wife, and be humbled under the mightie hand of the Lord. It is a mighty hand, and the Lord will be honoured, either in your Humiliation and converfion, or elfe in your damnation for ever. Let all the evill that is threatned, and all the good that is offered prevaile with your hearts, and though meanes cannot, yet the Lord prevaile with you: the Lord empty you, that Chrift may fill you, the Lord humble you, that you may enjoy happineffe, and peace for ever.

FINIS.

Oftober 10.
1637.

Imprimatur
T. Wykes.